Sing Musicals

A History of Singapore Musical Theatre

A History of Singapore Musical Theatre

Kenneth Lyen

NEW JERSEY · LONDON · SINGAPORE · BEIJING · SHANGHAI · HONG KONG · TAIPEI · CHENNAI · TOKYO

Published by

World Scientific Publishing Co. Pte. Ltd.
5 Toh Tuck Link, Singapore 596224
USA office: 27 Warren Street, Suite 401-402, Hackensack, NJ 07601
UK office: 57 Shelton Street, Covent Garden, London WC2H 9HE

Library of Congress Cataloging-in-Publication Data
Names: Lyen, Kenneth, author.
Title: Sing musicals : a history of Singapore musical theatre / Kenneth Lyen.
Description: Singapore : World Scientific Publishing Co. Pte. Ltd., [2023] |
    Includes bibliographical references and index.
Identifiers: LCCN 2023031048 | ISBN 9789811279508 (hardcover) |
    ISBN 9789811272448 (paperback)
Subjects: LCSH: Musicals--Singapore--History and criticism. |
    Musical theater--Singapore--History and criticism.
Classification: LCC ML1751.S5 L94 2023 | DDC 782.1/4095957--dc23/eng/20230705
LC record available at https://lccn.loc.gov/2023031048

British Library Cataloguing-in-Publication Data
A catalogue record for this book is available from the British Library.

Supported by the National Arts Council

NATIONAL ARTS COUNCIL
SINGAPORE

Copyright © 2023 by Kenneth Lyen

All rights reserved.

For any available supplementary material, please visit
https://www.worldscientific.com/worldscibooks/10.1142/13536#t=suppl

Typeset by Stallion Press
Email: enquiries@stallionpress.com

About Kenneth Lyen

Kenneth Lyen is a music composer, writer of books, and a consultant paediatrician.

He started composing music since he was 13 years old. He has composed over 200 songs for 33 musicals that have been staged in Singapore. For three of these musicals he also wrote the script. He co-wrote the music for Singapore's National Day Parade in 1997 and his songs were aired nationwide on television and radio.

He composed the music for MediaCorp's 6-part TV Musical *School House Rockz* which was televised in 2008. It was successful so a second series was written and produced in 2009, followed by *School House Rockz the Movie* which was broadcast in 2011. He composed half the songs for another MediaCorp Okto TV series for children, *Witz*, which was broadcast in 2011.

Over the years Ken has helped tertiary institutions young musicians, playwrights and filmmakers develop their composing and writing skills. From 2010 to the present, he has been involved in the teaching of writing musicals for Raffles Hall undergraduates at the National University of Singapore. He has also been involved in the incubation of new musicals for Musical Theatre Ltd since 2010.

He has co-authored 16 books on the mental health of children, parenting, intelligence, and he has written articles for several magazines.

Ken founded the Rainbow Centre that helps disabled children and individuals on the autism spectrum. For this he was awarded the public service star in 2022.

Dedication

This book is dedicated to:

My wife, Dr Huang Yuen Chin
My son Dr Stephen Lyen, his wife Dr Claudia Hon, and their children Max and Chloe
My daughter Claire Lyen, her husband Benjamin Phipps, and their children Elizabeth, Joseph and Jude
My sons Paul and Brian

They have all supported me in writing this book.

Foreword

I thank my multi-talented friend, Dr Kenneth Lyen, for inviting me to write the foreword of his path-breaking book on the history of the musical in Singapore.

I have spent more than twenty years of my life in America. I lived in New York City for thirteen years. One of the joys of living in New York was enjoying the wonderful shows on Broadway.

The Americans have excelled in producing musicals. I often wondered whether Singapore would produce our own musicals. The answer came in 1988 when three remarkable Singaporeans, Michael Chiang, Dick Lee and Ong Keng Sen, produced Beauty World. It was a hit. The success of Beauty World has led to a succession of wonderful musicals, in the English language. It is safe to say that the musical has taken root in Singapore.

For several years I wondered whether any of my friends would produce a musical in the Chinese language. My question was answered in 1996, with the production of December Rains. I saw a later edition with Kit Chan playing the note of Li Qing. I also saw Lao Jiu, in 2005 and Liao Zhai Rocks, in 2010. The musical has also taken root in the Chinese-language cultural world.

I am glad that Dr Lyen has a chapter in his book on "famous personalities". These are the pioneers who have led the way: Dick Lee, Stella Kon, Goh Boon Teck, Iskander Ismail (deceased), Liang Wern Fook, Ong Keng Sen, Ivan Heng, Selena Tan, Elaine Chan, Bang Wenfu, Michael Chiang, Kuo Jian Hong, Julian Wong and others.

I congratulate Dr Kenneth Lyen for having written a very comprehensive history of the musical in Singapore. I wish the book great success.

Tommy Koh

Preface

The history of the Singapore musical is fascinating because not only does it portray what Singapore was like in the past, but it also captures its cultures and languages. The first musicals appeared in 1988 and for the next two decades there was a flourishing of new musicals. But since 2010 there was a slowing down in new productions.

And then came the COVID-19 pandemic where Singapore responded aggressively by restricting movements, only allowing small groups of people into shops, eating places, offices, and educational institutions. Closure of theatres caused musical theatre to come to a crashing halt which lasted for two entire years.

In 2014 I was invited to write the chapter on "Singapore Musical Theatre" in the book *Singapore Soundscape*, edited Jun Zubillaga-Pow and Ho Chee Kong. The current book updates and expands on the history of the Singapore musical, tracing its ups and downs and analysing the many challenges it continues to face. It portrays many of the musicals staged publicly, and also the biography of the major creators. The final chapter explores some ideas on how we may be able to overcome the decline in new productions over the past decade, and how this artform can flower again.

I am one of the few people fortunate to have been able to watch the majority of Singapore musicals, and I have also written some of these musicals in collaboration with outstanding teams. So I am writing about the history of the Singapore musical from first hand experience. I have tried to include as many musicals as I can remember, but inevitably I will have left out some of them. Perhaps a future publication can plug the gaps. Some of the information in this book has been obtained from the internet and inevitably there may be inaccuracies or mistakes despite double checking the information. Please accept my apologies.

Ultimately my objective for writing this book is to keep a historical record of Singapore musicals and to promote the creation of future musicals. I hope to have sparked some interest in Singapore's creative arts and culture.

Thank you for reading the book.

Kenneth Lyen
July 2023

Acknowledgements

I would like to thank the following for their support in writing this book, and for granting me permission to publish their pictures and photographs:

Bang Wenfu
Elaine Chan
R Chandran
Chen Zhangyi
Amy Cheng
Felix Cheong
Michael Chiang
Goh Boon Teck
Henry Heng
Ivan Heng
Ganesh Kalyanam
Stella Kon
Gaurav Kripalani
Professor Tommy Koh
Kuo Jian Hong
Dick Lee
Liang Wern Fook
Jonathan Lim
Karen Lim Bjerg
August Lum

Dezz Desmond Moey
Shaifulbahri Mohamad
Ong Keng Sen
Desmond Sim
Erna Sorianto
Joel Tan
Selena Tan
Julian Wong
Frankie Malachi Yeo
Act 3 Theatrics
Dream Academy
Mascots and Puppets Specialists
Musical Theatre Ltd
National Arts Council
Sing'Theatre
Singapore Repertory Theatre
T>Works (formerly TheatreWorks)
The Theatre Practice
Toy Factory
W!ld Rice

Contents

About Kenneth Lyen — v
Dedication — vii
Foreword — ix
Preface — xi
Acknowledgements — xiii

Chapter 1   What is a Singapore Musical?   1
Chapter 2   English Language Musicals   7
Chapter 3   Non-English Musicals   51
Chapter 4   Pantomimes   65
Chapter 5   Operas   81
Chapter 6   School and University Campus Musicals   95
Chapter 7   Movie and Television Musicals   109
Chapter 8   Famous Personalities   115
Chapter 9   Developing New Singapore Musicals   153

Index   163

1 What is a Singapore Musical?

Arrival of Singapore Musicals

Singapore musical theatre is a relative latecomer compared to musicals from Europe and the USA. The first musical with music, lyrics and book entirely written and performed by Singaporeans in Singapore was *Makanplace* in 1988[1]. This was followed a few months later by Dick Lee's *Beauty World*[2]. Both were influenced by Broadway and West End musicals.

Prior to that, all the musicals performed in Singapore were imported from Europe and the USA. There are some possible reasons why new Singapore musicals took so long to germinate. The British who governed Singapore from 1819 until 1963 were the main drivers of music and theatre productions, and not unnaturally they tended to choose the ones they were familiar with. But even from the time when Singapore gained self-government in 1959 followed by independence from UK in 1963, only established western musicals were performed in Singapore, presumably because production companies felt it was safer economically to cater for an established audience base, rather than risk exploring an untested local show.

During the first two decades after independence, the Singapore financial resources were precarious and it was not until the 1980's that the Singapore economy blossomed, so that by the 1990's the gross domestic product rose dramatically to about US$13,000, surpassing South Korea, Israel, and Portugal[3]. The flourishing economy bolstered local confidence, and it coincided with a new generation of artists willing to experiment with new art forms.

Mega-shows like *Phantom of the Opera* and *Miss Saigon* have mega-budgets with each show requiring several millions of dollars to produce. One advantage that Singapore has is that the cost of a production is still relatively low. A modest musical can be mounted at around S$750,000 or less.

For the two decades after the launch of Singapore's first two musicals, *Makanplace* and *Beauty World*, around two to four full-fledged musicals have been produced each year[4]. This contrasts with the 40 plus musicals mounted annually in Broadway and the West End during the same period. Singapore musicals usually run for about two weeks on average, while successful musicals in the USA and England can run for several months or even years. Singapore's audience size for musical theatre is relatively small compared to western countries, and this may be related to the lack of a strong tradition of theatre attendance. It translates into short runs and unfilled seats, which in turn means greater difficulties in generating income and finding investors. One also suffers from the "prophet-not-recognized-in-one's-own-land" syndrome. Imported goods (and musicals) are considered superior to indigenous stuff!

Musical theatre is a collaborative artform requiring several layers of integration. On the creative side, there is the amalgamation of music, lyrics, book, choreography, etc. On the performance side, the participants need to be able to act, sing and dance. On the production side, the producer must be able to coordinate all these aspects and find an acting director, a music director, a choreographer, a lighting director, sound engineer, and backstage manager. Finding outstanding directors, choreographers, performers, musicians, lighting and sound designers, etc., remains a perennial problem. Often one has to import some of these professionals. Assembling all these team members increases the budget, which translates into higher ticket prices and deters audience attendance.

All the above factors contributed to the delay in mounting Singapore musicals.

Influences on the Singapore Musical

Singapore is at the crossroads between the East and the West. The musical theatre influences are mostly from USA, Europe and Australia on the one hand, China, Japan and Korea on the other, and perhaps to a lesser extent, India, Middle Eastern, and African countries.

Most Singapore musicals are written in English because of the heavy influences of Broadway, West End, and the Hollywood musicals showcased in cinemas and the live stage. English language musicals continue to dominate the landscape, and it is only relatively recently that Chinese language musicals like *Snow Wolf Lake* (1996), *Lao Jiu* (2005) and *Sometime Moon* (2018) have emerged.

Singapore writers and composers, not bounded by West End or Broadway traditions, are more willing to experiment. Indeed, the success of *Makanplace* and *Beauty World* sparked a series of local musicals largely influenced by Asian stories, culture and Singlish (Singaporean English). With the added benefit of being a highly computer- and multimedia-savvy country, there is now a combination of both eastern and western influences together with computer technology. Already the newer musicals are beginning to take advantage of all these influences.

A few musicals, like *Chang and Eng* (1997) and *Beauty World* (1988), have traveled overseas. It is the ambition of theatre companies to bring more productions overseas, and hopefully one day reach the two Meccas of musical theatre, namely, Broadway and the West End.

Since around 2010, musical theatre attendance in Singapore has declined, in part it is because of the rise in ticket prices owing to the increased cost of staging a musical, and in part because of a loss of public interest in musicals. This decline is worldwide, and even Broadway musicals became less sought after.

Then in 2020, COVID-19 struck a shocking blow to the theatre industry. Crowds were not allowed to assemble, international travel was brought to a standstill and there were no tourists. For almost two years theatres were closed, and restrictions were only eased towards the end of 2021. In 2022 tourists started coming back and theatres were allowed to take in more audiences. Recovery continues to gain momentum, and a number of newly-written Singapore musicals have appeared on the scene. This has taken the form of using regional stories and blending Asian with western music.

Chinese opera had been declining in the past few decades, but with the reopening of theatres after the COVID-19 pandemic, there has been a spark of rediscovery with the production of *wayang* or Chinese opera-style musicals embracing ancient folk tales and creating original music that blends Chinese music using traditional instruments with western-style music arrangements. Attendance has been increasing, especially with the younger audience.

Modern technology has also made inroads into musical productions. For example, staging has been contemporized using backdrop projections creating an immersive reality which augments one's experience.

Musical theatre remains an essential art form with important spin-offs in community bonding, the promotion of a creative industry for a creative city, and there is considerable cross-fertilization with other related industries including multimedia, film, and animation. In Broadway and the West End it is a profitable tourist attraction. The problem is that musical theatre remains one of the most expensive stage productions, and therefore to rejuvenate this art form, it needs to be actively supported. It will be interesting to watch how the Singapore musical will continue to evolve.

Definition of the Singapore Musical

What is a Singapore musical? Here are some issues open for discussion.

1. Written by a Singaporean

Must a Singapore musical be written by a Singaporean? Must it be about Singapore? Can a non-Singaporean write something about Singapore? The 2015 musical *Singapura* was written by a Filipino, Ed Gatchalian, who was not a Singaporean. Although the characters are Singaporean and it is set in Singapore, the cast members are Filipinos, and the production does not capture the Singapore atmosphere or identity of the country or its people. The lack of this spirit resulted in a negative public reaction and a call by some critics to reject *Singapura* as a Singapore musical. However, it is currently listed as a Singapore musical.

Stephen Clark, a British playwright and librettist contributed significantly to three of Singapore's musicals, *Sing to the Dawn* (1996), *Forbidden City* (2002), and *LKY Musical* (2015). The music was written by Singapore's Dick Lee and the cast was mostly Singaporean. The public response to these three musicals was favorable and they have embraced them as Singapore musicals.

An exception is the musical *Puteri Gunung Ledang* which has music composed by Singaporean Dick Lee, but it still remains a Malaysian musical.

2. Set in Singapore

Does a Singapore musical have to be set in Singapore? The musical *Chang and Eng* (1997) is about two conjoined Siamese twins and it is set in Thailand and the USA. The songs were written by Ken Low and the book was written by Ming Wong, both Singaporeans, so this musical is considered Singaporean.

Other Singapore musicals set outside Singapore include the Mandarin dialect musical *If There're Seasons…* (2009) which is about the Singaporean overseas community in New York, and Dick Lee's musical *Forbidden City* (2002) about the Empress Dowager is set in Beijing. Should they be regarded as Singapore musicals? The consensus opinion suggests that yes, they should.

3. Contains Singapore Culture, Story or Features a Singaporean Character

Should a Singapore musical have a Singapore theme, a Singapore story, or features a Singaporean? For example, should the characters speak Singlish or Singapore English? It is argued that the absence of colloquial dialect, the omission of Singapore culture, story or even a Singaporean main character does not necessarily exclude the musical as being Singaporean.

There does not appear to be 100% consensus on any of the above points and there will always be naysayers who argue against any proposed definitions of the Singapore musical. It shows how difficult it is to define what exactly is a Singapore musical. In the end it may be best to subscribe to a "rojak" (eclectic mix) approach in defining a Singapore musical. One might try to embrace a little bit of everything: perhaps one member of the creative team should be Singaporean, but this is not an absolute rule; perhaps it should include a Singapore theme or story, or perhaps it should capture some of the ethos, character, and culture of the country. In the final analysis, the stories should resonate with Singaporeans, and should ideally be of universal appeal. That is probably what constitutes a Singapore musical. But ultimately, the definition of a Singapore musical might end up being any production that claims itself as such.

Singapore musical theatre is a relatively young artform, but over the decades it has gradually been gaining popularity. By writing about regional stories and characters, and blending Asian cultures into the production styles, it is now attracting larger audiences. Hopefully it will continue to evolve and become established as the hallmark of Singapore, and recognized worldwide.

References

1. Atkey, Mel. A Million Miles from Broadway: Musical Theatre beyond New York and London. Toronto: Friendlysong Books, 2019. ISBN 0991695747
2. Hales, Aaron. 'The State on Stage: A Socio-Political Critique of Singaporean Musical Theatre.' Ph.D. Dissertation, School of Music and School of Social and Cultural Studies, University of Western Australia, 2009.
3. Lee, Dick. The Adventures of the Mad Chinaman. Singapore: Marshall Cavendish, 2011. ISBN 9812326022
4. Lyen KR. Singapore musical theatre. In *Singapore Soundscape* edited by Jun Zubillaga-Pow and Ho Chee Kong. National Library Board, 2014. ISBN: 9789810792688
5. Menon R. An economic history of Singapore — 1965–2065 https://www.bis.org/review/r150807b.htm
6. Report of the Advisory Council on Culture and the Arts. Singapore, 1989.
7. Tan, Kenneth Paul. Renaissance Singapore: Economy, Culture, and Politics. Singapore: National University of Singapore Press, 2007. ISBN 9789971693770 https://scholarbank.nus.edu.sg/handle/10635/151293
8. Yeoh, Lizhen Geraldine. 'The Singapore Musical: Perspectives, Paradigms, Practices.' Honours Thesis, Department of Theatre Studies, National University of Singapore, 2011. https://scholarbank.nus.edu.sg/handle/10635/49631
9. Perera LM, Perera A. Music in Singapore: From the 1920s to the 2000s. National Library Board Singapore 2010. https://docslib.org/doc/5694253/music-in-singapore-from-the-1920s-to-the-2000s-by-perera-loretta-marie-and-perera-audrey-written-in-august-2010-national-library-board-singapore

2 English Language Musicals

Most of the original Singapore musicals are written in English for several reasons. The British ruled Singapore for one and a half century, leaving a government, legal, educational and exam system using English. In a multiracial multilingual society, English was regarded as a neutral language among the Chinese, Malays, Indians and other races in Singapore. Furthermore, when it came to international trade, English was the lingua franca that enabled worldwide communication.

Singapore gained self-government in 1959, and the next year, in 1960, compulsory bilingual education was introduced by the government. Although the Chinese formed the majority of Singapore's population, and most of them spoke Hokkien, when bilingual education was introduced, the Chinese taught in schools was Mandarin, which only a minority of the population spoke. Therefore Mandarin felt more like a foreign language, comparable to the way English was regarded. However, Singaporeans found it easier to write in English rather than Chinese. Many of the new books, plays, poems, and song lyrics were written in English. During this period there was a strong emphasis on science education and most science textbooks were published in English, which further elevated the status of English.

When Singapore gained independence in 1965, the government introduced four official languages, namely, English, Mandarin, Malay and Tamil. However, English remained the language of government as well as the legal system, so it continued to be the dominant language.

Early theatre companies were set up by the British, and they tended to import plays and musicals from the West End plus a few from Broadway, and hence the Singapore public was exposed to this culture.

Western influences also extended to popular music such as pop rock, jazz, and more recently hip-hop and rap. Even the Japanese and Korean popular music, J-pop and K-pop, sound very much like western pop music. Not surprisingly, the style of music for most Singapore musicals is western pop. The first Singapore musicals are *Makanplace* and *Beauty World*, both produced in 1988, have western influenced songs.

Makanplace (1988)

Makanplace has the distinction of being the first Singapore musical to be staged, in 1988. The book was written by R. Chandran, the music composed by Jasmin Samat Simon and Saedah Samat-Alkaff, and the song libretto was written by Jasmin Samat Simon. The production company was Act 3 and it was directed by R. Chandran, with Richard Tan doing the choreography. "Makan" means "eat," and in the local context it refers to a hawker center where the musical is set. The story follows the lives of two teenage schoolboys Siew and Zil. Siew is infatuated with his mentor a female tutor, while Zil dreams of entering the show business. The hawkers are having problems trying to pay the debt collectors, and in order to make ends meet they raise the price of their food. Another element of the musical is the rivalry between the all-girls and the all-boys school students who are regulars of the hawker center. The musical captures the neighborhood's informal lifestyle, vernacular speech and unsophisticated humor. *Makanplace* was first produced in 1988 and a made-for-television version was aired by

Singapore Broadcasting Corporation in the early 1990s. It was restaged by Republic Polytechnic in 2012. The latter production had some excellent singing, the dancing is well-choreographed, and the humor quite hilarious. It remains a timeless classic.

Beauty World (1988)

Beauty World (1988) was staged at the World Trade Centre Auditorium a few months after *Makanplace*. Michael Chiang wrote the book with music and lyrics by Dick Lee. It was produced by TheatreWorks, directed by Ong Keng Sen and choreographed by Najip Ali. The story is set in Singapore in 1965, and follows Ivy Chan Poh Choo, an illegitimate child who was abandoned by her family in smalltown Batu Pahat, Johor, Malaysia. The only clue to her origins is a fragment of a jade pendant with the words "Beauty World" inscribed on its back. She travels to Singapore to look for her biological father, and first visits her eccentric pen friend, who tells her that Beauty World is actually a sleazy nightclub in Singapore. Undeterred, Ivy goes to this dicey establishment where she meets several people including the main cabaret dancer Lulu, nightclub manager Mummy who is the "mother" running the place, Ah Hock, a youthful gangster bartender, and Boss Quek, the owner of the club. To increase the chances of finding her father, Ivy decides to work at the nightclub, but one of the regulars, Towkay Tan, lures her into a room upstairs and tries to rape her. Fortunately, she is saved by Ah Hock, who is attracted to her. At the end of the musical, Ivy finds out who her parents are, but her relationship with Ah Hock is left uncertain. There is a liberal use of Singlish (Singapore English) which the local audiences enjoy and laugh lustily. Dick Lee's music is melodic with a style out of the 1950s. The most memorable tunes are *Beauty World Cha Cha Cha*, *Single in Singapore*, *Another World*, and *Ivy*. In 1992 it went on tour in the Japanese cities of Fukuoka, Hiroshima, Osaka and Tokyo. In 1998, it was reproduced as a television musical production for the President's Star Charity. *Beauty World* is a landmark musical for Singapore.

Fried Rice Paradise (1991)

Fried Rice Paradise was originally produced by Singapore Repertory Theatre in 1991 but was completely rewritten in 2010 by Dick Lee to celebrate the 50th anniversary of the People's Association. It is a musical comedy set in the 1970s during a time when Singapore was modernizing and some of the older businesses were unable to survive. The story centers on Bee Lean, who is trying to save her father's coffee shop from being bought over by Rickson Goh, the next-door owner of a disco joint who wants to expand his entertainment nightspot. She is also trying to save their entire row of shophouses from being repossessed by the authorities. Bee Lean's idea is to transform her father's coffee shop and attract more customers by producing her mother's famous fried rice recipe. Unfortunately, the plot takes a bit too long to set up, and the insertion of community songs in the first half seems a bit forced. The most memorable song is *Fried Rice Paradise*. The other catchy song is the *Mahjong Song* which reflects Bee Lean's zest for this game. The script is funny and there is a liberal use of Singlish, and subtly implied jokes like the name of the private investigator labeled as Inspector Chao "kaypoh" which is slang for busybody.

Kampong Amber (1994)

The musical *Kampong Amber* was specially written for the Singapore Festival of Arts in 1994, and was staged at the Kallang Theatre. The book

was written by Catherine Lim, music and lyrics by Dick Lee. Set in the 1930s it is about Jimmy Koh, a village boy who wants to discover a more exciting life outside the kampong. The village beauty, Ah Choo, is in love with Johnny but he is not interested in her. One day, Jimmy saves the life of the millionaire Lim Kia Hock who owns a villa nearby, and is invited to work for him. There he encounters Mr Lim's daughter Peggy, and it is love at first sight. But Peggy's mother has already arranged with a matchmaker for Peggy to marry someone wealthy, namely Philip. However, Philip is attracted not to Peggy, but to Mr Lim's second wife, May. In the meantime Mr Lim wants to buy and redevelop Kampong Amber, but faces considerable resistance from the villagers. A fierce fire burns down the entire village and initially Mr Lim was blamed. To everyone's surprise the culprits who set fire were caught holding kerosene cans and matches. It turns out they are Mr Lim's second wife May and her lover Philip, whose motive is to get Mr Lim convicted for the criminal act of igniting the fire so the two can get married. Mr Lim is shocked by their act, and informs the villagers that he will no longer be buying their kampong. He also promises to compensate the villagers for their losses and that he will rebuild their kampong. At the end of the musical, Jimmy proposes to Peggy. As usual, Dick Lee's music is tuneful, and perhaps the most memorable are *Bunga Sayang* ("Flower of Love"), and the theme song *Kampong Amber*.

Big Bang! (1995)

Big Bang! the musical was staged at the Kallang Theatre in 1995. The script was written by Stephen Yan, the lyrics by Desmond Moey, and the music by Kenneth Lyen and Desmond Moey. Additional music was written by Adrain Oh. It was directed by Bob Turoff. The story is based on the life of Cambridge cosmologist, Stephen Hawking, represented by Peter Morris, who is trying to understand the origin of the universe and proposes the Big Bang theory. To arrive at this theory, he explores the ideas proposed by other historical figures and he travels through the history of astronomy from the ancient Chinese, through Galileo, Isaac Newton, Albert Einstein and Fred Hoyle. Peter Morris falls in love with Anne, his university colleague, but when he discovers he is suffering from an incurable terminal illness, he becomes totally obsessed with his work and pays no attention to Anne. But she is deeply in love with Peter, and feels very lonely when he ignores her. Only later, when he meets an Einstein figure who advises him to appreciate love and look for a deeper meaning in one's life, that Peter Morris realizes his shortcomings. Memorable songs include *Big Bang!*, *I like Your Mind* and *Stars*. The music was also used during the official opening of the research building Fusionopolis in 2008, with Prime Minister Lee Hsien Loong in attendance.

Corporate Animals (1995)

Corporate Animals book was written by Desmond Sim, with music and lyrics by Ken Low. The show was directed by Ekachai Uekrongtham of Action Theatre. *Corporate Animals* depicts a large company as a jungle where staff "animals" are fighting for supremacy. It features a middle-rung staff member, David, who is working for Veronica, a venomous viper. On his first day of work, she tells him in a song that he can either be a *Leader or a Ladder*, suggesting that as an inert ladder others will exploit and climb on top of him. The clever use of dance allows the different members of the corporation to adopt the behavior of one of the animals they represent. The song and dance number *Jungle in Here* has a powerful beat that makes you want to dance along. The beautiful ballad, *Simple Days*, has strong lyrics and is sung by David's girlfriend June. In the end David and June tearfully come back together again and decide not to be part of the jungle any more. The acting, singing and dancing strongly support the storyline.

Mortal Sins (1995)

Mortal Sins the musical is a collaboration between Michael Chiang who wrote the book, and Dick Lee who wrote the music and lyrics. It was produced and directed by Ong Keng Sen of T:>Works (formerly TheatreWorks) with choreography by Najip Ali. It was staged in Kallang Theatre with a capacious set and a large projected screen in the centre. The plot revolves around two ladies: Rosie, a stripper from the 1960s, and Jackie Atria, a contemporary moralist who sits on the Singapore censorship board and wants to protect the younger generation from vice and corruption. Upright Jackie wakes up one day to find herself time-transported back into the 1960s and she is inside a brothel, where she meets Rosie. In the song *Dreams* they sing about their common dreams of making Singapore a lively rich artistic city. The song *The Nineties* depicts a prosperous dynamic place. The chorus members are dressed in black, initially in the sleazy 1960s as nightclub dancers with suggestive sexy movements. Later they are depicted as a mob who will try to determine the moral equilibrium of society. In the meantime Jackie maintains her high moralistic stance and she sings *Cut, Cut, Cut* using scissors to show that she believes in strict censorship. When Rosie tries to follow Jackie's advice to follow her dreams, the brothel's Mama San disfigures her by splashing acid onto her face rather than allowing her to go free. In the song *Waiting*, we learn that Jackie's value system has evolved and she is no longer so high-minded and more liberal with censorship. But when she looks for Rosie, she finds that she has passed away. In her final words from the grave, Rosie tells the audience that making money and becoming prosperous is not the ultimate goal, but that it is a mortal sin not follow your heart and discover the true meaning of life. The songs carry the storyline very well.

Sing to the Dawn (1996)

Sing to the Dawn (1996) was produced by the Singapore Repertory Theatre and staged at the Kallang Theatre. Based on the novel of the same name, the script was written by Ho Minfong and Stephen Clark, with lyrics by Stephen Clark and music by Dick Lee. It was directed by Steven Dexter and choreographed by Gani Abdul Karim. *Sing to the Dawn* is the story of Dawan, a Thai peasant girl who wins a scholarship to study in the city but has to overcome parental and societal gender discrimination in order to achieve her educational goal. The story explores the deep emotional conflicts both within and outside the family. Dawan's father wants her to marry their neighbor's son, and to tutor her younger brother so that he can win the scholarship and she can therefore remain in the village. Mother uses the fear tactic of highlighting the perils and vices of 'The City' to dissuade Dawan from accepting the scholarship, and this is depicted in a scene showing Go-go dance girls, pimps and prostitutes. Dawan is resolutely determined to stand up to discrimination against females, and she succeeds. The music captures the ethnic character of Thailand and covers a wide range of moods. Three songs stand out: *The City*, *It Just Flies* and *My Child*. The musical is unrelated to the 2008 animation with the same title and story.

Chang and Eng (1997)

Chang and Eng (1997) was written by Ming Wong with music and lyrics by Ken Low. It was directed by Ekachai Uekrongtham of Action Theatre, and choreographed by Mohd Noor Saman. The story is based on the real lives of a pair of conjoined Siamese twins, Chang and Eng (1811–1874) who lived to 62 years of age, both dying within hours of each other. The musical starts off in their childhood where they are living in Thailand and earn their living by selling duck eggs. They are mocked by other children and are blamed for a cholera outbreak in their village. An unscrupulous merchant chances upon them and takes them to America where he makes them part of a freak show and exploits them. Unfortunately, the twins are cheated out of their earnings, and have no money to return to Thailand. They meet a pair of American twins with whom they fall in love, marry and produce a total of 21 children. The musical explores the problems of people living in extremely close proximity and how they need to give and take. This is expressed in the tear-jerking theme song *Mai Phen Rai*, meaning "it's

okay" and the beautiful song is repeated several times. The other songs that Ken Low wrote varied from the comic *The Grand Midwife of the West* to the touching ballad *From Now On*. The show was a commercial success and toured China, Hong Kong and Thailand.

A Twist of Fate (1997)

Commissioned for the 100th anniversary celebration of Raffles Hotel, the story of *A Twist of Fate* was written by Steven Dexter and Tony Petito, lyrics by Anthony Drewe, music composed by Dick Lee, and was premiered in Jubilee Hall of Raffles Hotel. It was produced by the Singapore Repertory Theatre. The story is about a baby abandoned in 1917 on the front steps of this famous hotel, and when found by a childless English couple, was adopted and brought back to England. Twenty years later, in 1937, the adopted girl named Emma West, is looking for her biological parents and writes to a Mr Lim Chin Boon, who coincidentally happens to be looking for his long-lost grand-daughter. But when Emma arrives in Singapore, she is plunged into a den of intrigue, hostility, and foul play. Old man Baba Lim Chin Boon the rich owner of a mansion, is murdered halfway through the show, and everybody becomes a suspect, including Emma. The other suspects include Mr. Lim's lawyer, who falls in love with Emma. We learn that Mr. Lim's second wife, Ming is scheming with Mr Lim's business associate, "Uncle" Albert. Ming's daughter, Alice, has fallen in love with their servant boy, Ah See, and her mother is vehemently against their secret liaison. Confused? This whodunit mystery is a traditional farce with many laugh-out-loud moments. There is an abundance of puns and clever wordplay. For example, when Ah See stomps off angrily and kills a chicken, he is said to be "in a fowl mood". And it was "inconceivable" that Mr. Lim could possibly be the father of his second wife's child. The plot is well constructed with enough red herrings, and unexpected twists and turns to keep one guessing all the way. Dick Lee's music is pleasant, functional, and fulfils its role quite well. The song *Killing Chickens* is hilarious, the ensemble song *At Midnight* is hummanble, and Emma's song *Who Am I* is heartrending and haunting. A revised version was restaged in 2005.

Haunted (1999)

The book was written by Mark Chan and Ovidia Yu, with music and lyrics by Mark Chan. Performed at Victoria Theatre it was directed by Casey Lim and produced by T:>Works (formerly TheatreWorks). It is a serious family drama punctuated with some humorous moments. Charles, the long-lost grandson of Grandfather Loong, has mysteriously returned to claim his place in the family. Also appearing at the same time is the ghost Lillian, who was the grandfather's mistress but had died mysteriously many years ago,

presumably killed. Appropriately haunting is the song she sings, *I Wake*, dressed in white, with lamps swaying and doors slamming. The central theme of this musical is about love and betrayal, where family secrets are gradually revealed, and this is echoed by the title song *Haunted*. The plot is rather predictable so it loses the audiences' attention. The story of this musical is "hauntingly" similar to another musical, *A Twist of Fate*; perhaps it was written for Raffles Hotel celebration but the producer did not choose this presentation, preferring Steven Dexter and Tony Petito's version which has a more unpredictable plot.

The Magic Paintbrush (2000)

The Magic Paintbrush is Singapore's first locally written, full scale musical puppet show with book and lyrics by Brian Seward and music by Kenneth Lyen. It was first produced at the Drama Centre. This musical is written for both children as well as adults, and the script is humorous and contains clever references to pop culture, including the movies "*Titanic*" and "*Jaws.*" The puppets were created by Frankie Yeo, Singapore's first professional puppet maker. They ranged from the cuddly singing flowers and chickens, to the gigantic towering spectre called The Spirit of Creation. *The Magic Paintbrush* is based on an ancient Chinese folk tale about a poor but talented painter who receives a gift of a magic paintbrush which enables him to paint things into life. Modifying this narrative, the story is set in Singapore and the artist is a young girl called Toni. She is pressurised by her father to excel in her science exams and not to waste time with her art. While taking a break from her studies she picks up a storybook, *The Magic Paintbrush* and meets the magic paintbrush. She accidentally makes a wish and with the aid of a faulty computer, she is transported back into ancient China where she helps some poor villagers by providing them with food and other basic needs. The cruel Emperor gets to know about the magic paintbrush and sends his incompetent guards Sotong and Shrimp to steal the paintbrush. Toni is captured and imprisoned and the Emperor becomes too greedy and when traveling on his royal boat he wishes it was made of gold, whereupon it sinks and he is drowned. The theme of the musical is about the value of friendship, helping the poor, the dangers of greed and abusing one's power, and the value of creativity. The musical has been restaged several times.

Chameleon (2000)

With music by Bang Wenfu, the book and lyrics were written by Denise Marsh, who also produced and directed the show, this musical was staged at Jubilee Hall in Raffles Hotel. Set in a discotheque *Chameleon* is a story about Ms Devine, a transvestite who tries to help others with similar transgender or LGBTQIA tendencies to come out of their closet. The musical depicts the colorful spectrum of the different characters and the central theme is sung by Ms Devine in the song *You Must be True to Yourself*. The music and dance is in the cabaret and Latino styles of the 1970s and

there are finger-snapping campy drag performances where the men are dressed as women and women as men. One of the characters, Marsh asks the audience "What's normal? You? And who are you to judge?" and two other characters, Pearl and Jade, bring up issues of feminism, femininity and masculinity through her song *Why Can't Men*. Towards the end, Jasper, the proprietor of the lounge and a closet homosexual, suffers from depression and attempts suicide but fails and is left paralysed. The final message is that you should accept yourself as you are, and you should not hide or keep on changing like a chameleon. There are a number of good songs, including *Latino Lover*, and *Sparkle*.

Temptations (2000)

Temptations (2000) was produced by the Rainbow Theatre. The script was written by Kenneth Lyen, with lyrics by Desmond Moey and music composed by Kenneth Lyen, Desmond Moey and Iskandar Ismail. The show was directed by Jonathan Lim and produced at the Neptune Theatre. The story is about newspaper food critic Shawn who takes Leila, his fellow reporter and girlfriend, to a high-class restaurant called 'Temptations'. But because

of their improper dress, the snobbish restaurant owner, Cat, treats them condescendingly. As a result, Shawn writes a poisonous article about the restaurant in his newspaper column. Cat subsequently turns up at Shawn's newspaper office to protest, but Shawn refuses to retract his article. Not long after Cat and her restaurant's cook go for drinks at a nearby café where they bump into Shawn and Leila again, and all four are forced to share a table. It slowly becomes apparent that behind the duelling words of Shawn and Cat is a subtext that they are actually enjoying each other's company. The unlikely pair gradually fall in love and a series of events draw them closer. There is a subplot concerning a cross-dressing cook and relationship with Leila. Four other actors make up a Greek chorus and act as intermediaries to the audience. The highlights of the musical are the songs that drive the plot forwards, including *No Slippers, No Shorts*, *Getting Burnt* and *Manya's Story*.

Women on Canvas (2000)

Jonathan Lim wrote the book and lyrics and Bang Wenfu composed the music to the musical *Women on Canvas*. Four women depicted in four oil paintings come out of the canvas and transform into living persons. The original paintings of these women are projected onto a screen. The first piece is an impressionist art but the woman who emerges from the painting is a glitzy beauty who objects to her portrait as being too fuzzy. The second is a young studious bookworm who transforms into a sexy adolescent. The third painting is in the style of Andy Warhol, and the woman talks about her actual wonderful meeting with Warhol and likes the separate depictions of herself. The fourth woman is one who has been abused by men and lives in fear of them. These women meet up and discuss their personal problems, and they also analyse their own portraits and discover their deeper inner character and they emerge more self-confident and wiser. Jonathan Lim's book and lyrics enhanced by Bang Wenfu's music explores the individual personalities of these four women and provides the show with its strength and vitality.

Sayang (2001)

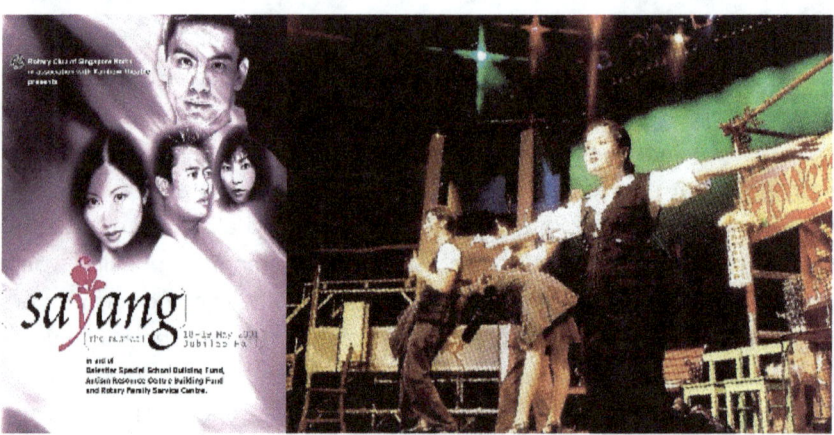

The book of *Sayang* the musical was written by Vincent Wong, with lyrics by Ivan Ho, and music composed by Kenneth Lyen. "Sayang" means "love" in Malay, and it centres around the relationship between Mike, a radio deejay who gives advice on love, and Raine, a flower shop girl. The story begins on Valentine's Day with lovers and lovelorn characters phoning in declarations of love to the radio station. Raine is in her flower shop when she hears Mike's voice on the radio, and she instantly falls in love with the voice, whereupon she sends him flowers from her shop. There is an intermediate scene set in an internet chatroom where people fall in love online in a song. Raine dials into the radio station, and talks to Mike on air, and publicly asks Mike out for a dinner date. He agrees and during their meeting they discover they both like each other and when Mike asks Raine if he can hug her, she says yes, but while hugging her he gives her a deep kiss. After a while, they break the kiss and Raine confesses that she already has another boyfriend. Mike pursues Raine, and their uncertain relationship is reflected in the songs sung with their close confidante friends. In the end Raine has to decide whether or not to accept Mike's love. Maybe from a distance? The songs carry the musical and transforms it into a light-hearted Broadway-style musical. Memorable songs include *Something Has Begun*, and *When You Fall in Love*.

Forbidden City: Portrait of an Empress (2002)

Forbidden City: Portrait of an Empress (2002) was commissioned to mark the opening of The Esplanade Theatre. The script was written by Stephen Clark and Dick Lee, with lyrics by Stephen Clark and music by Dick Lee. The musical draws from Sterling Seagrave's controversial biography of Empress Dowager Cixi. The actual Forbidden City refers to the imperial palace complex located in the heart of Beijing. The story narrates the Empress' struggle for survival behind the closed doors of this Forbidden City, and how she maintains her power in the face of calumny from her own subjects as well as misreporting by the British press. The story is told from the point of view of an American portrait painter, Kate Carl, who is sympathetic to the Empress, but when she relays her accounts to an unscrupulous British journalist George Morrison, he distorts the narrative and stigmatizes the Empress as an evil tyrant. There is comic relief provided by the two Record Keepers. The Empress is played by three different actresses portraying the young, middle-aged and elderly dowager. The Empress' brother-in-law, Prince Tun, is an ambitious scheming rival to the throne. However, he is killed during the Boxer Rebellion and on his death the ensemble sings a haunting ballad. The music is pleasant and enhances the drama. Memorable songs include *Land of My Fathers*, *My Only Chance*, and *Blood in the Streets*. Forbidden City was restaged in 2003, 2006 and 2017.

Re:Mix (2002)

Re:Mix is a musical with songs by Dick Lee set in a disco and the overall theme is what takes place when teenagers go clubbing. The musical starts off with bouncers stamping attendance on the teens' wrists while the throbbing rock music is being played. A rotating silver disco ball hangs in the middle of the stage and scatters light directed at it. The young cast acts out the different relationships and behaviours ranging from having fun, approaching and making new friends, drinking alcohol, becoming jealous when someone takes away their partner. Throughout the show is the pounding dance music. The underlying theme is the exchange of innocence for awareness of the painful reality of love and its loss.

Shanty (2004)

Produced by T:>Works (formerly TheatreWorks), the book and lyrics of *Shanty* were written by Robin Loon and the music composed by Henry Chua who was one of the founding members of the 1960s Singapore rock band, The Quests. "Shanty" was the title of the instrumental smash hit of The Quests in 1964, and indeed the musical is inspired in part by The Quests' journey. It starts off when four passionate teenagers decide to get together to form a band and enter Singapore's Talentime competition, hoping to gain fame and success. The band wins the championship and they go on to produce four number one hits, and even manage to bump off the Beatles from the number one spot on the Singapore charts. All four band members had joined the group hoping to escape from their underlying personal problems, but once they achieve success beyond their wildest dreams, they become overconfident and their inner demons give rise to a series of conflicts. For example. one of the members has a mother who had recently walked out of the family, and he himself becomes a ladies' man flirting with girls. Another has an abusive father and he becomes a gang member. One of the band members is married and decides that his marriage is more important and decides to leave the group, resulting in an irreversible breakup of The Quests. Ultimately *Shanty* is a tale of lost innocence and broken dreams. The 1960s style of pop-rock toe-tapping music is very infectious.

Phua Chu Kang (2005)

Phua Chu Kang (2005) was staged at the Kallang Indoor Stadium. The script is unaccredited; the lyrics were written by Edmund Ooi, Catherine Casey, Vivienne Lin and Adeline Tan, and the music composed by Edmund Ooi and

Peter Casey. The show was directed by Edmund Ooi and choreographed by Bill Calhoun. It was produced by MediaCorp Studios. The main character of the show is Phua Chu Kang, a contractor who is on the brink of turning 40. He makes profuse hints to his relatives and workers, but they all pretend to be ignorant while secretly they are arranging a surprise birthday party. In the meantime, Phua Chu Kang's arch adversary, Frankie Foo, is furious that Phua Chu Kang had stolen his childhood girlfriend Rosie and pledges revenge. He sends one of his relatives, who resembles Phua Chu Kang, to claim to be his long-lost brother, Chu Kok. Chu Kang is totally deceived by this imposter, who takes him to see a Feng Shui master. In the form of a rap, the latter informs Chu Kang that he will die on his 40th birthday. Depressed, Chu Kang signs away his house and entrusts all his belongings to the fraudulent brother. Chu Kang's family is infuriated that everything has been given away to this trickster. Just as the villainous Frankie Foo is about to claim Phua Chu Kang's home and evict the entire family, he has a heart attack. Phua Chu Kang resuscitates Frankie, who then tears up the contract, but secretly vows to destroy his savior in the future. The script could have been tightened with removal of dances that did not advance the plot, and the performance did not live up to expectations. The organizers boasted that the show cost S$3 million to produce, making it one of the more expensive musicals in Singapore.

Lost In Transit (2005)

Written by Stella Kon and music by Desmond Moey, *Lost In Transit* was performed at the Arts House which has a small but intimate theatre which

English Language Musicals

was appropriate for this show. The musical centres around Mia, a simple village girl, who is tempted into the big city with dreams of becoming a singing superstar, only to be led into a life of vice. Her fiancé Sam goes to the city in search of her, and finds that she is being raped and harmed by a rich tyrannical businessman. Trying to save his girlfriend, they fight but Sam accidentally stabs the rapist, and ends up in jail. Mia's grandmother, the proverbial wise old lady describes Mia and Sam as 'lost in transit'. This sad musical is adorned with really beautiful songs and memorable melodies including: *Hear the Song*, *And I Will Always Love You*, and the song where Mia sings about losing her way in life, *There is a River*. The unexpected ending is difficult to reconcile.

The Admiral's Odyssey (2005)

The Admiral's Odyssey was written by Jean Tay, with lyrics by Ken Low and Jean Tay, music composed by Ken Low, and produced by Action Theatre. This musical is about a young boy, Chris Cheng who discovers a footprint belonging to the 15th century Chinese explorer Admiral Cheng Ho. Suddenly, as if by magic, Admiral Cheng Ho appears in front of young Chris and briefly recounts his travels. A few years pass by and Chris has grown up into a young man, and he has fallen in love with Lily. But when he asks

her to follow him globetrotting, she declines. Chris leaves behind Lily, his doting dressmaker mother, and his elder brother Colin, while he follows the same routes that Admiral Cheng Ho took six hundred years ago, except he travels mostly by airplane. Chris is away for quite a long time, and his travels do not go to plan. So reluctantly, he decides to return home whereupon he learns that his mother has suffered a serious illness. But by the time he reaches home, it is too late, and his mother has already passed away. Furthermore Lily, his girlfriend, has married his elder brother Colin. The book contains many jokes, including a visual one, with Admiral Cheng Ho holding a copy of the book "1421, The Year China Discovered America", which works out as 71 years before Christopher Columbus landed there. However, the story is not really about Admiral Cheng Ho, but more about Chris, a prodigal son returning home who does not offer any penance nor receive any forgiveness. The final message this musical conveys is that you might go round the world seeking for meaning in life, but what you are searching for is actually at home all along. The songs are melodic and the final song with Admiral Cheng Ho, *Will You Remember*, starts off with an Asian arrangement, but after the first few bars rapidly abandons the Asian style and enters a contemporary Western idiom. As a 600th anniversary celebration of Admiral Cheng Ho's voyage, it is a pity that this musical contains too little narrative about this distinguished ancient explorer.

Georgette (2007)

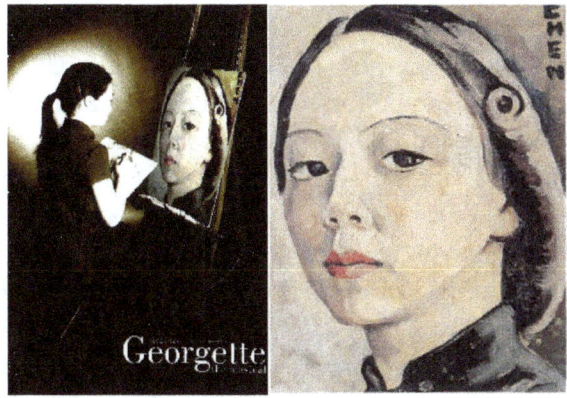

Georgette (2007) was produced and staged at the Esplanade Recital Studio by Musical Theatre Ltd. The script and lyrics were written by Ng Yi-Sheng and the music by Clement Yang. The musical is about the life and times of pioneer Singapore artist Georgette Chen. The first half focuses on her younger formative years and her relationship with Eugene, an ethnic Chinese from Trinidad who is twice her age and eventually becomes the foreign minister of China. Georgette is fiercely independent while Eugene is reserved. Nevertheless, they marry against the wishes of Georgette's wealthy parents. The story follows the pair as they travel from China to Paris to Trinidad, and when they are back in China they are ultimately caught up by the sweep of history. They are imprisoned by the Japanese who have occupied Shanghai during the Second World War and they encounter the Chinese communist forces. Eugene dies in captivity and at his burial, Georgette remembers his last wish which was for her to do a self-portrait. And when her father tells her that she should not be thinking about art, her answer is "There is always time for art." She moves to Singapore as an artist and devotes her life to painting. The music reflects the different countries and periods very well. It is one of the more innovative Singapore musicals with intelligent humorous dialogue and song lyrics. Memorable songs include *Woman on the Wall*, *Don't Cross Your Chopsticks*, *Raise the Flag*, and *A Bowl of Fruits*. *Georgette* the musical is an authentic account of the life of Georgette Chen, and the show was also staged in the Philippines. This is a first-rate musical.

It's My Life (2008)

The musical's book was written by Chong Tze Chien, with lyrics by Lim Yu-Beng, and music composed by Bang Wenfu. Directed by Lim Yu Beng, *It's My Life* was produced by Tan Kheng Hua's theatre company A Spare Room, and was staged at the National University of Singapore's Cultural Centre in 2008. It is about ten teenage auditioneers who have already been chosen to perform in a show where they each have to sing, dance and talk about their own life stories and their dreams. This story echoes the Broadway show *A Chorus Line*. While the latter maintains tension because of the elimination process of auditions, *It's My Life* lacks this competitive pressure. For example, one of the cast members talks about their dream "to study art," but the moment the teenager faces an obstacle, they abandon their dreams. There is a scene where the students are listening to their mobile device, and another where they are describing themselves online using their laptops. What makes the musical enjoyable is the youthful enthusiasm and the lively dancing that invigorates the production.

H is for Hantu (2009)

H is for Hantu (2009) is a musical comedy originally staged at the Alliance Française Auditorium. The script and lyrics were written by Jonathan Lim and the music was composed and directed by Bang Wenfu. Giant puppets were designed, created and manipulated by Frankie Malachi Yeo. The show was directed by Jonathan Lim and produced by his company Stages. Sazali is a schoolboy who can see "hantu" (the Malay word for "ghosts"). He is living in Singapore's last remaining kampongs, where a community of spirits lives nearby. When Angie Seah, a woman from the Housing Development Board, comes to evict the residents so that the kampong can be redeveloped into government flats, Sazali decides to fight the bureaucrats. However, it turns out that Angie is a victim herself, possessed by an unspeaking ghost who drives her to scramble through the jungle at night, searching for something. Sazali investigates and finds out that Angie used to live in that kampong as a child and her best friend, Swee Choo, a mute girl, died soon after her departure for city life. It comes to light that Angie is not the villain and actually fought hard to be the director of the kampong's relocation so that she could ensure the residents were treated decently and optimally. Since one cannot defeat the Government once it has made up its mind, it would be more pragmatic for Angie to get the best deal possible for the residents. When Angie gets an offer for attractive new apartments, the residents are happy to move and ultimately they keep their community together using a Facebook group. Angie eventually meets the ghost of Swee Choo face-to-face and presents her with the token of their friendship that Swee Choo had been searching for. The best thing about the show might be the puppets, which are spectacular. The music supports the mock spooky feel of the musical. In the end, the musical is about friendship lost and found, and that home is where your heart belongs. Happy ending. The musical was restaged in 2011.

Sing Dollar! (2009)

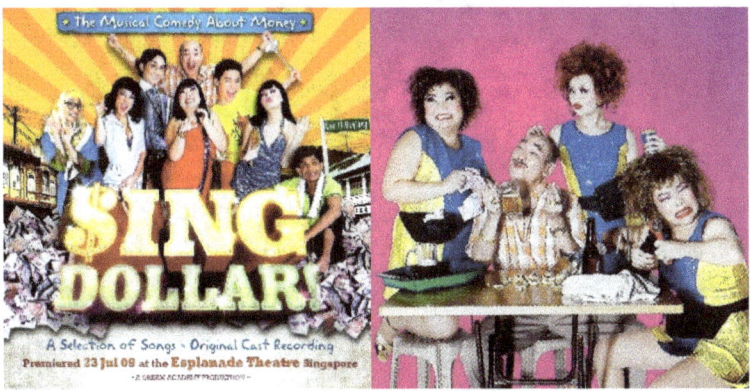

The book and lyrics of *Sing Dollar!* were written by Selena Tan, and music by Elaine Chan. Produced by Dream Academy, it was staged at the Esplanade Theatre. Set during a global financial crisis, this music comedy starts off with a maid stumbling upon a dead body in a hotel room situated in Singapore's dubious red light district of Geylang. Six more people turn up, curious to find out what happened to the dead person. This includes an uncultured Ah Beng who operates a beef hor fun noodle stall, his illegal immigrant Bangladeshi migrant worker who is in love with a Filipino domestic helper, his slick yet guilt-ridden banker brother, a Tiger Beer auntie, and a prostitute from China. Then unexpectedly a trash bag falls down from the ceiling and is found to contain half a million Singapore dollars. When they see the money, all seven people want it. To justify why they deserve the money, each one tells their individual life story through song and dance. They also reveal their greed, their guilt, and their questionable integrity. The humour is slapstick, and some of the song lyrics combine English, Chinese and Malay. Somehow the moral of the story where integrity and family ties should triumph over monetary greed seems to have evaporated during the show. Well, that's real life!

Sleepless Town (2009)

Written by Mark Richmond, the music was composed by Don Richmond and Jason Tan, and directed by Beatrice Chia-Richmond, and produced by Toy Factory. *Sleepless Town* the musical is about Nora, a troubled teenage girl who goes to a mysterious fantasyland called Sleepless Town. It is a wild chaotic world ruled by Black Azira, an evil queen, who wants to gain immortality by stealing the citizens of their dreams which will actually kill them. To block Azira, Nora secures the help of several superheroes, including the Flying Fox who is the facsimile of Batman, and Sparrowman who is a pseudo-Robin. She also gets hold of The Incredible Bulk who is grossly overweight and without the muscles of The Incredible Hulk. In reality these superheroes are quite useless because they do not have any superpowers, and indeed they themselves need to be helped in the end. Nora eventually learns that she has to fight Black Azira single-handedly. But first, she has to struggle against her own personal demons, such as her sexual problems. Up to this point, the musical is a fantasy comedy. Then, quite out of the blue, Nora's stepfather attempts to rape her, and mother protects Nora by killing her rapist husband. The abrupt change in mood catches the audience off guard. The story is narrated by Aristotle who tells it in the style of a rap. There are some interesting songs, like one that features historical villains, including Hitler, Saddam Hussein, and Osama bin Laden. Nora sings a beautiful song with a nice melody, *I'll Find My Way*. The musical ends with Nora having a supernatural reunion with her biological father, and they sing a compelling duet *With Love*, which is about the healing power of love.

So You Want to be a Nurse (2012)

The book and lyrics of *So You Want to be a Nurse* were written by Justin Kan, and the music was composed by Kenneth Lyen. The musical is set as a game show titled "So You Want to be a Nurse," where contestants compete with one another to become the top nurse. The annual champion has always been won several times by veteran Nurse Choo. The new challenger who has reached the finals is young Stacy, fresh out of nursing school, and she introduces herself singing *Calling*, and we learn that her mother strongly disapproves of her going into the nursing profession. The contestants have to go through three rounds set in a hospital. The first round for Stacy involves looking after Cici, a young child with cancer, and Stacy volunteers to talk to her when her mother leaves the ward to speak to their doctor. Cici tells Stacy through a song that her mother promised she will be a ballerina when she grows up, and while she sings a ballerina appears in the background dancing beautifully. Cici's mother returns to the room informing Stacy of the bad news concerning her daughter who is terminally ill, and not long after Cici passes away. Stacy is devastated and regrets having chosen nursing in the song *Any Other Job*. She loses round one. In round two, they have to draw blood from a grumpy old patient who is throwing a tantrum and refuses to have his blood drawn. Amazingly, Nurse Choo manages to get the blood drawn by forcibly tying her patient to the bed post so that he cannot struggle. Stacy fails and decides to quit the game show. Startled by her decision to leave halfway through the show, the host quickly calls for a commercial break. Then someone passes Stacy a drawing by the late Cici showing a picture of herself as a grown-up nurse. Several patients thank Stacy for the help she has shown. This changes Stacy's mind and she returns to the game show. The last round is decisive, and requires the contestant to go through a curtain behind which is a patient who might be suffering from a deadly infectious disease, and the song for this round is *The Final Curtain*. Nurse Choo decides not to enter the isolation room and throws in the towel, while Stacy bravely walks right in. The games host then announces that the winner is Stacy. They all sing *So You Want to be a Nurse*, followed by *Calling*. Overall the performance is excellent, and the entire cast are triple threats, able to sing, dance, and act superbly.

Lightseeker (2014)

Lightseeker is written by Andrea Teo with music by Dick Lee and performed in the Resorts World Theatre at Sentosa. Set in a magical universe, it is

about an evil General who wants to serve his nefarious emperor by making him more powerful. He comes across a mysterious girl called Nova, who has the ability to create The Light. The battle between good and evil is fought out between the dark General and the good people of his empire led by Nova. This is the main thrust of the plot, and it is the jaw-dropping sets, the breathtaking acrobatics of the troupe, and the tempestuous music and songs that carries the entire musical.

LKY (2015)

This hagiographic biographic musical of Lee Kuan Yew (LKY) the first prime minister of Singapore was written by Tony Petito based on a biographical history by Meira Chand, lyrics were written by Stephen Clark, and music composed by Dick Lee. Produced by Metropolitan Productions, it was presented at the Marina Bay Sands Theatre. *LKY* the musical paints a panoramic history of Singapore from the 1940s until its independence in 1965. During the second world war it shows LKY's quick-thinking to escape from the Japanese, and during his university days in Cambridge it captures the tenderness of his love for his wife Kwa Geok Choo. After the war the musical shows his charisma as leader of his political party that confronted the British and later opposed the communists. Lim Chin Siong, the left-wing trade unionist and a co-founding member of the People's Action Party, is initially supported by LKY but when he is labeled as an instigator of violent protests, he loses support and is imprisoned. The Malaysian prime minister Tunku Abdul Rahman is portrayed as a poker-playing politician, whose initial opposition to Singapore's desire to merge with Malaya to form Malaysia makes him another antagonist. If it is possible to write a historical musical where the ending is known at the outset, and yet manages to maintain a degree of suspense right to the very end, *LKY* succeeds amazingly. However, there is a problem with *LKY* the musical in that it covers too wide a period of history where much of the action and historical figures are dealt with somewhat superficially. But as a musical for Singapore audiences, it is impactful.

Singapura (2015)

Produced by 4th Wall Theatre Company, the book and lyrics of *Singapura* were written by Joel Trinidad and the music was composed by

Ed Gatchalian, both from the Philippines. It was directed by an American, Greg Ganakas. The story is set when Singapore was still under British rule and follows its road to independence from 1950s to the 1960s as seen through the eyes of a family living through this period. The story revolves around the Tan family, comprising father Kok Yang, a Hock Lee Company bus driver, mother Bee Ling who runs a kopitiam (a local coffee house), and their daughter Lee May. Their lives and dreams are caught up with the vicissitudes of destiny. Headstrong Lee May is attending law school and is a student activist. She falls in love with Flynn, a British officer, and they sing a love duet *Be With Me*. Unfortunately she is caught up in a love triangle between Flynn and her childhood Malay friend, Adam. The two males represent the confronting political sides that Singapore was caught in between. Father fears the dangers of living in Singapore where there are violent demonstrations, and he wishes to move to Malacca which he thinks is safer. The prime minister of Singapore is not named but simply referred to as "The Man in White," and from his classic pose, one knows who he is. The music is highly commended: it is strident during the turbulent scenes, romantic during the courting scenes, sad when the mother dies, and triumphant when she rises from her death bed to symbolically ascend the staircase to a better place. Other hummanble tunes include *Another Day in Singapore*, *At The Kopitiam*, *Moving Forward*, and *Tomorrow Begins Today*. Most of the creative team and cast were non-Singaporeans, and the majority of Singaporean reviewers wrote that the sentiment of this musical felt un-Singaporean. Pity the creative and production team did not consult local opinions.

Nanyang (2015)

Nanyang the musical was written by Alec Tok, lyrics by Eric Ng and music composed by Xiaohan. It is loosely based on the lives of five famous Singapore Nanyang artists, but none of them were named. Actually, the reviewer could deduce that the big five artists are Georgette Chen, Liu Kang, Cheong Soo Pieng, Chen Wen Hsi and Chen Chong Swee. Georgette Chen is referred to as Li Ting in the musical, and Liu Kang as Chen Kang. It starts off in Shanghai during the second world war just before the Japanese occupation of China. The plot is confusing: Li Ting (Georgette Chen) has enrolled in the Xinhua Art Academy in Shanghai when she drops her purse which is returned by fellow male Chen Kang (Liu Kang). He is immediately attracted to her and spends the rest of the musical chasing after her. In real life there is no such attraction. Their art instructor Zhang Wen successfully auctions one of his paintings which is apparently controversial, but the audience never sees the painting, so cannot gauge how controversial it really is. Then quite abruptly Chen Kang, Li Ting and four other art students inexplicably decide to go to Paris which is under Nazi occupation. In Paris, two classmates, Ren Hao and Yue Ping announce their plans to get married and to spend their honeymoon in Bali. Coincidentally Chen Kang and art instructor Zhang Wen have also decided to travel there. In the meantime, Li Ting announces that she is going to America. In Bali, we discover that Zhang Wen is already married to a Balinese dancer, Nini, and they already have a young son. Then Zhang Wen receives a letter from Li Ting announcing that she is now in Singapore. So they all decide to converge onto Singapore and meet Li Ting. Unfortunately on arrival, the Japanese have just occupied Singapore and they happen to know about the controversial painting, so they have a warrant to arrest Zhang Wen. Initially Chen Kang pretends that he is Zhang Wen. Upon realizing that the Japanese intend to shoot the painter, Zhang Wen gives himself up, whereupon he is immediately shot. The other artists survive the Japanese occupation and remain in Singapore and make a name for themselves after the war. The songs are sung in English, and the music styles include mandopop, xinyao, and Balinese music. The melodies are reasonably good, and the danceable music is backed up by flutes, violins, drums, guitars, and ethnic instruments. The plot rambles and does not sustain one's attention. Chosen to be part of the 2015 Singapore International Festival of Arts, Nanyang the musical is a let-down.

Emily (2016)

Emily's story has been transformed into a musical with a script written by Stella Kon and songs by award-winning composer Desmond Moey, and produced by Musical Theatre Ltd. Instead of having a solo actress as in the original play, "Emily of Emerald Hill", the musical includes a modest-sized cast of glittering Nonyas and Babas of the 1930's. The music conveys their pains and passions, and the colourful Peranakan love of life. *Emily* the musical focuses on Emily's struggle to find self-worth and love. Although her family was initially well-off and privileged, its fortune plummeted, so Emily chooses to elevate her status by marrying into the wealthy Gan family of Emerald Hill. With diamond-hard determination she works her way up to becoming a powerful matriarch, dominating the lives of all around her, especially her son Richard, and her husband Kheong. When the musical opens, an elderly Emily is being asked by her children to move out of her beloved mansion at Emerald Hill. She looks back on her life, her quest for status and influence. The rousing opening march *Welcome to Emerald Hill* shows the lavish entertainment of the heyday of the Peranakans and the ensemble number *Nonya Besar* celebrates Emily's status as the mistress of Emerald Hill. The touching song *Mother and Child* expresses the bond between Emily and her son Richard. Her husband Kheong sings a beautiful ballad to his mistress, Diana Lee, avowing that she is the only one who can *Awaken My Slumbering Heart*. By the end of her life, Emily finally acknowledges that with all her scheming and manipulation, *Love Was All I Wanted*. She realises this too late.

My Love is Blind (2017)

In 2016 Musical Theatre Ltd presented the premiere of *My Love is Blind*, a new musical based on the semi-autobiographical novel written by Tan Guan Heng. An experienced playwright, Leon Foo, was commissioned to create a libretto from Guan's novel, with music composed by Julian Chua and additional lyrics by Kevin Seah. In the musical, protagonist Guan finds his life upended when he is left blind after a university hockey accident. The story follows his journey as he picks himself up and finds his way in the world. Buoyed by a colourful cast that includes both blind and sighted people, it becomes a sparkling heartfelt musical full of humour, with a touching love story, and reaching heights that one does not expect. Guan joins what was then known as the Singapore Association for the Blind (SAB), where he learns the tools to manage his new life and he meets new friends along the way. He also finds himself falling for a nurse who helps him back on his feet. With a newfound belief in himself, as well as the support of his eccentric family and quirky friends, Guan achieves new milestones in his life: he opens his own bookshop, becomes the first blind president of the SAB after a string of sighted presidents, and finally finds his true love. Songs include the poignant *In the Morning the Sun Will Rise*, the gentle ballad *My Love is Blind*, and the stirring *Let the Blind Lead the Blind*, as Guan campaigns to be elected as the first blind president of the Blind Association. *My Love is Blind* is a very inspiring story about human courage and determination, and it carries a strong social message about what the disabled, including the visually disabled, are able to achieve.

Tropicana (2017)

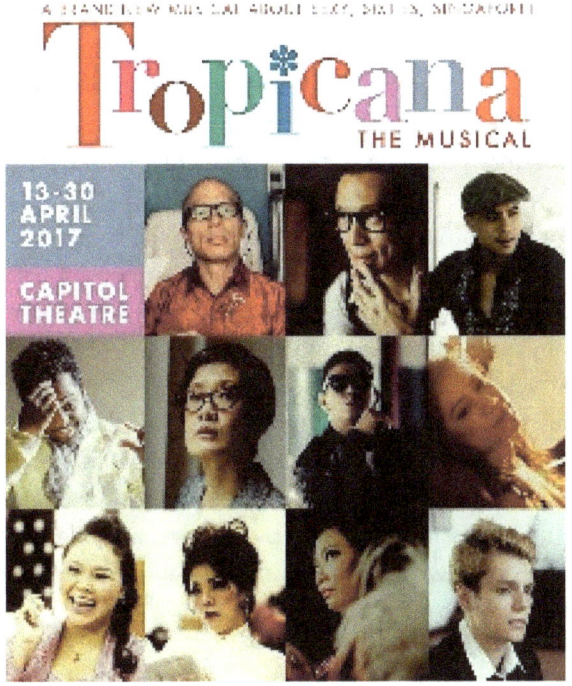

The book of *Tropicana* the musical was written by Haresh Sharma, lyrics by Joel Bertrand Tan and music composed by Julian Wong. It is set in the popular 1960s and 1970s Tropicana night club, well known for its topless dancing. The Singapore Tourist Promotion Board, a government statutory board, was instrumental in setting up Tropicana, which is ironic, because in the 1970s the squeaky-clean authorities would send police raids or plant plain-clothed police spies inside the premises. The story is largely based on historical events that include the starting of the actual Tropicana nightclub, which ran into some problems when it became too popular and rather too profitable. A mafioso wanted to be made a partner, but was declined by Tropicana's owner, Reggie. The gangster sent some thugs to physically harm some of the Tropicana staff in an attempt to persuade the owner to offer him a partnership. The musical also recounts the 1969 race riots in Singapore which were sparked off by the 13 May incident in Kuala Lumpur. At around the same time there was a rise in hippie culture of the 1970s which was characterized by long hair, promiscuous lifestyle, and drug use. Reacting to this, Singapore banned long hair, did not allow psychedelic rock music to be played in nightclubs and public places, and disallowed broadcasting of songs whose lyrics were deemed to evoke drug use. The combination of the 1969 race riots and the rise of hippie culture led the authorities to tighten up on all arts and entertainment performances and publications. The severe censorship devastated Singapore's film, theatre and other arts industries in the 1970s. The brilliance of *Tropicana* the musical is that it manages to encompass these important historical events in the form of an entertaining revue and expressed in a heartfelt manner. There are many memorable scenes. One of them is while singing a ballad on stage the background shows the silhouette of violent fighting between the Tropicana staff and the gangsters. The flames showing the final days of the Tropicana when it caught fire are incredibly stunning. Memorable songs include *Live Your Life*, *Tropicana*, *Send Me a Dream* and *A Time for Everything*. The musical can be seen by some as a subtle commentary on the politics of the era when arts and entertainment and expressive freedoms were subdued.

Pinocchio (2017)

The book and lyrics of the puppet musical *Pinocchio* were written by Desmond Sim, with music composed by Kenneth Lyen, and puppets by Frankie Malachi Yeo. It was performed at The Pavilion in Far East Square. The story is based on the 1883 story of Pinocchio created by the Italian writer Carlo Callodi where the puppet becomes transformed into a real boy. Unlike the Disney version of Pinocchio, the story starts with Pinocchio and Naggity, his cricket companion being swallowed by the whale while they are searching for his creator-father, Gepetto. By chance, Gepetto has also been swallowed earlier by this whale, and so they are reunited inside its belly. The story continues as a flashback. To underline the environmental message, the audience are seated inside a giant whale constructed out of 40,000 plastic bottles collected by school children. The singers are all excellent and includes a 9-year-old playing the role of Pinocchio. Two visually impaired singers play the roles of Gepetto and Naggity the Cricket. The book and lyrics play a critical role in characterization and storytelling, so when Pinocchio realizes he can move and talk, he sings *I'm Alive!*. There is a comic banter song between Pinocchio and the wise cricket, *Naughty and Naggity*. Gepetto displays his fatherly love of the puppets he created in the song *My Little Children*. The wily deceiving Fox and Cat smooth-talk their way in *Your Best Friend*.

Several messages are being conveyed by this musical, including the famous one where one should not tell lies because one's nose will elongate like Pinocchio's. The second message was triggered off by the 2015 news of a dead sperm whale discovered in Singapore waters near Jurong Island. The cause of the whale's demise was due to the swallowing of vast quantities of waste plastic wrappers and cups. Hence preventing plastic waste and protecting life on the planet was a powerful message embedded in *Pinocchio* the musical. The use of puppets in a musical lends itself to incredible imagination, great humour, dynamic energy and powerful emotions.

Itsy (2017)

The musical *Itsy* takes its title from the nursery rhyme The "Itsy Bitsy Spider". Chong Tze Chien wrote the script and the music was composed by Darren Ng. This puppet show was produced by The Finger Players and staged in Victoria Theatre. There are two threads to the story. The first is grandfather

Gong Gong who is suffering from dementia, desperately trying to help his grandson Xavier who has fallen into a coma. In his dreams, Xavier lives in a land of nursery rhymes where he is free of pain, and he rules the kingdom as Young King Cole. The second thread involves Itsy, the spider, who is disliked by everyone because his adhesive cobwebs is gluing up their lives. Upset by being ostracized, Itsy takes revenge by amassing an army of fellow spiders to launch a war against the nursery rhyme characters. They attack Humpty Dumpty, the Three Blind Mice, and Jack and Jill. By taking a bite on their victims, the spider robs them of their memory. To protect these characters and to prevent their loss of memory, grandfather tells them to keep on singing their personal nursery rhyme again and again. This technique can also be applied to the grandfather himself because he is getting increasingly demented. Then Gong Gong tells his grandson that only through pain can he escape from his coma. Xavier replies affrontedly: "How can pain fight pain?" Grandfather convinces him that they must all team up to battle the spiders, and eventually their friendship and love conquers all, and Xavier comes out of unconsciousness. This is a clever borrowing of real-life medical strategy because doctors have found that patients with dementia or children suffering from anxiety sometimes see giant shadows of spiders on their walls, which creates fear and jogs them back into normality. Supported by scintillating puppetry and lively music, *Itsy* is a powerful story about the love between a grandparent and his grandchild.

Lim Boon Keng (2019)

Lim Boon Keng the musical was written by Stella Kon, his great grand-daughter, and the music was composed by Desmond Moey, and it was produced by Musical Theatre Ltd. The life of Lim Boon Keng (1869–1957) is a very complex one, and the story spans from his being awarded the Queen's scholarship to study medicine at Edinburgh University in 1887, until his death in 1957. The musical starts and ends with the trial of Lim Boon Keng for treason because he was accused of being a spy and collaborator with the enemy during the Japanese occupation of Singapore in World War II. Although he was eventually legally cleared of the charges, all his friends ostracized him because his reputation had been stained. The musical can be divided into several segments. One concerns his marriage to Margaret Huang in 1896, but she passed away quite early in 1905. The story continues with the marriage to his second wife Grace Yin which lasted from 1908 until Lim Boon Keng's passage. He was a strong advocate of democracy and he was elected to the Legislative Council of Singapore, and he supported the British war effort during World War I, for which he was awarded the Order of the British Empire. He also supported Sun Yat Sen's revolution in China. A third part of his life follows his support of women's education where he fought hard to set up the Chinese Girls' School in Singapore, and later he became the president of Amoy University in China. Culturally, Lim Boon Keng promoted the peranakan heritage to which he belonged, and he also advocated bilingual education in Singapore. To weave together these multiple strands of philosophies, emotional conflicts, and historical events in Lim Boon Keng's life, is potentially quite confusing. But thanks to astute writing, together with creative production teams, they managed to pull it off. The show also looks at Lim Boon Keng's interaction with the local community, and his efforts to bring them into the future. The music captures the many shades of emotions exhibited by the characters, as well as the changing historical and geographic landscapes most appropriately. There are memorable songs that poke fun at the Peranakan lifestyle, like *Merci Buku* and the ode to *Sambal Belachan*. The musical honours Lim Boon Keng's accomplishments as a pioneering father of Singapore, but also recognizes his struggles and challenges which made him who he was.

Tissue Aunty (2022)

Tissue Aunty the musical was produced, directed and choreographed by Mario Chan who also wrote the book, the lyrics, and composed the music. It was quite a shock to learn that he passed away just a couple of days before the premiere of his musical. The show follows Zac, a student whose mother is ill and he decides to sell packets of tissue paper to earn money to pay for her medical bills. He chooses Bedok, an area where three aunties claim is their territory to sell tissue paper. For trespassing on their domain, they tie him up, imprison and interrogate him asking where he got his tissue paper from. When two of the aunties go off to sell tissue paper, the third auntie left to watch him, takes pity on him when she learns of his mother's illness, and she not only teaches him how to sell tissue paper but also lets him go free. In the meantime, one learns that his mother is actually not ill, and that she is also involved in selling tissue paper to her own gang. The plot is full of humorous unexpected twists and turns. The songs are melodic and danceable, and reinforce the characters personalities as well as the story line. The singing and acting is arousing and comical. The lyrics utilise Singlish and embed local humour, like "We will tissue a lesson" meaning "we will teach you a lesson". Non-Singaporeans may not realise that the mention of buying sugarcane drink with extra lemon refers to the deputy prime minister's speech during the 2020 general elections. The opening song *Three One Dollar* and the closing song *No No No* are catchy and lively, and the song *The Heart Goes* is poignant. *Tissue Aunty* would have been a great start to Mario Chan's writing career if he were still around. Rest in peace.

Paiseh Pieces (2023)

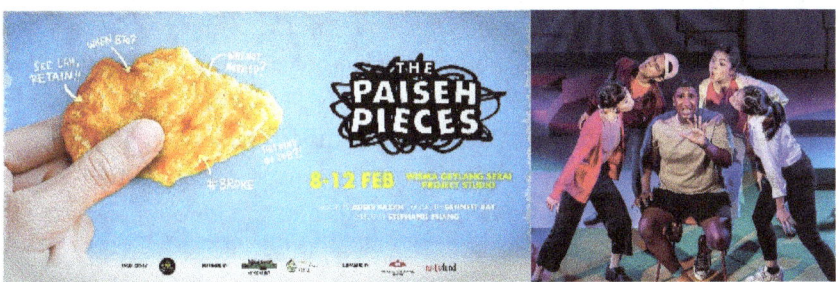

Written and directed by Adeeb Fazah, with music composed by Bennett Bay, lyrics by Stephanie Phang and produced by The Second Breakfast Company, *The Paiseh Pieces* is a highly polished energetic musical with a dash of humour sprinkled throughout the script. It was staged in 2023 at the Wisma Geylang Serai Project Studio. We follow three friends who have recently graduated from university, each with a story to tell. The first is Sarah who has a boyfriend Johan, and he has put their names down to buy a Built To Order (BTO) flat. He keeps on delaying proposing marriage despite hints by Sarah who points out that in Singapore, priority of allocating BTO flats is given to couples who are registered in marriage. Johan's consistent delays upset Sarah and she begins to seriously wonder if she should continue her relationship with Johan. The second story is about Tobias who graduated from the university drama course and when he is called up for auditions, he is hopeful that he can pursue a career as a stage actor. To his dismay he is consistently rejected by many theatre companies, and he comes to realise that perhaps he may find better prospects if he took a Master's degree overseas, like Canada. The third person followed is Rina who is repeating a year at university but loves animals and wants to devote her life looking after animals. Her mother who is the sole breadwinner is struggling to make ends meet, and wishes that Rina would pursue a more lucrative career. She also wants to help Rina in the event that she passes away, they can avoid paying estate duty by putting Rina's name as co-owner of the flat that she owns. But Rina is uncomfortable taking on extra responsibility at this time in her life. She joins an animal sanctuary organisation and is working very long hours and underpaid, which stresses her out. Overall, the acting and singing is first class and carries the emotions very powerfully. The choreography is well-synchronised and very exciting. However, there are a few concerns about this musical. The problems faced by the three main characters are not satisfactorily resolved at the end. The title is unsatisfactory because the Hokkien word "paiseh" is a lighthearted resigned way of expressing one's slight embarrassment, mild shyness, or a sense of shame when doing something a bit unconventional. The journey of the three plotlines are too serious and too emotionally intense to fit the title "The Paiseh Pieces". However, this musical is an important resurrection of the Singapore musical that has lain dormant for three years during the COVID-19 pandemic. It is very professionally produced and it is an entertaining musical.

The Monster in the Mirror (2023)

Originally premiering in 2021 online because of theatre restrictions during the COVID-19 pandemic, Gateway Arts' *The Monster in the Mirror* is back as a stage production. It is a musical written and directed by Terrance Tan, music composed by Michelle Ler, lyrics written by Cheryl Chitty Tan, and with artistic direction by Samantha Scott-Blackhall. This is a humourous yet serious musical about the psychological journey of Jane, a teenage girl tracking through a tortuous path lined by school bullies and a nagging mother while she tries to maintain her sanity. She keeps on hearing voices in her head that torments her by criticising everything she does. One day she receives a magic mirror from a flashy Fairy God Delivery Beng played by the popular *Ah Boys to Men* star, Noah Yap. When she stares into the mirror she sees the monster who has been residing in her head and has been torturing her mind by giving her self-doubts. The Monster tries to take over her mind, but the more Jane tries to combat it by refusing to admit her failings, the worse it gets. Only when she learns to accept who she really is, flaws and all, that she begins to control the Monster, and learns to forgive and love herself. During the show, you also learn more about Jane, and that she is an excellent artist, and that she has to tolerate a mother who does not understand her emotions, and also when she has to fight against a mean classmate bully who is a social media influencer. The songs bring the musical to new heights, accompanied by excellent singing and dancing. The multimedia back-projections are used to animate Jane's drawings, and also to illustrate what Jane sees on her mobile phone as well as her emotional reactions. The Monster in the Mirror is an important musical as it reflects the stresses and aspirations of the younger generation, and empowers them to deal with mental health.

References

1. Lyen KR. Singapore musical theatre. In Singapore Soundscape edited by Jun Zubillaga-Pow and Ho Chee Kong. National Library Board, 2014. ISBN: 9789810792688
2. Oon, Clarissa. Theatre life: a history of English-language theatre in Singapore through The Straits Times (1958–2000). Singapore Press Holdings (2001) ISBN 9810437056

3. Yeoh, Lizhen Geraldine. 'The Singapore Musical: Perspectives, Paradigms, Practices.' Honours Thesis, Department of Theatre Studies, National University of Singapore, 2011. https://scholarbank.nus.edu.sg/handle/10635/49631
4. Lee, Dick. The Adventures of the Mad Chinaman. Singapore: Marshall Cavendish, 2011. ISBN 9812326022
5. Menon R. An economic history of Singapore — 1965–2065 https://www.bis.org/review/r150807b.htm
6. Report of the Advisory Council on Culture and the Arts. Singapore, 1989.
7. Tan, Kenneth Paul. Renaissance Singapore: Economy, Culture, and Politics. Singapore: National University of Singapore Press, 2007. ISBN 9789971693770
8. Alfian Sa'at. Twenty Years of W!ld Rice (2023). Epigram Books. ISBN: 9789814845885

Websites Archives

1. Centre42 Archives: https://www.centre42.sg/
2. W!ld Rice Archives: https://www.wildrice.com.sg/
3. TheatreWorks Past Productions: https://theatreworks.org.sg/cover/home.htm
4. Singapore Repertory Theatre Past Productions: https://www.srt.com.sg/past-productions-and-licensing
5. Musical Theatre Ltd Past Productions: https://mtlmanager.wixsite.com/mtl5/our-histor

3 Non-English Musicals

In its early years, all original Singapore musicals were written in English; it is only from the mid-1990s that Chinese-language musicals gradually made their appearance. Despite being performed either entirely in Chinese, or a mixture of different Chinese dialects with English, the structure and style of Chinese-language musicals reflect Broadway and West End musicals. The exceptions are the musicals that incorporate the xinyao Mandarin folk-song style of music pioneered by Liang Wern Fook in the 1980s. These are melodic songs without the heavy beat of contemporary western pop music and are ideally suited for romantic or melancholic stories. Some of the recent Chinese musicals being staged are influenced by traditional *wayang* or Chinese street opera, either modifying an ancient folk tale or using melodies and Chinese instruments combined with western musical forms. The most prominent names in the production of original Chinese-language Singapore musicals are Goh Boon Teck and Kuo Jian Hong.

Malay operatic theatre is known as *bangsawan* and was developed in the early 20th century. This is performed in several countries in Southeast Asia, including Malaysia, Indonesia, Singapore and Thailand. Its popularity has waned over the past few decades. Original Malay language musicals have been produced mostly in Malaysia and only one from Singapore. The popular Malay musical *Puteri Gunung Ledang* has music composed by Singapore's Dick Lee. Other Malay musicals include *Hoore! Hoore!* which is a movie musical directed by Saw Teong Hin, *Magika*, a musical film directed by Edry Abdul Halim, *Rock*, and its sequel *Rock Oo* produced by Mamat Khalid, and *Leftwings*, directed by Faisal Chal Ahmad.

Indian musicals are popular especially as part of the Bollywood movies. In 2013 Andrew Lloyd Webber invited AR Rahman to write a musical in English but using Indian music and it had the title *Bombay Dreams* which was very successful in the West End. In 2022, the long-running Indian movie musical, *Dilwale Dulhania Le Jayenge* also known as *DDLJ* was adapted and staged on Broadway. The script was written by Aditya Chopra and the music composed by Jatin and Lalit Pandit. In 2023, the popular Bollywood musical Devdas was adapted into a stage musical and premiered in Singapore. So far there are no new Indian language stage musicals written by and produced by Singaporeans.

Titoudao (1994)

Toy Factory Productions founder Goh Boon Teck wrote, produced and directed *Titoudao* the musical in the style of a *wayang* or Chinese street opera as a tribute to his mother, Oon Ah Chiam. In her younger days in the 1940s Singapore, Oon was a famous Chinese opera singer, and the story follows her real life experiences when she journeys from a kampong girl and becomes a famous *wayang* celebrity, and then later becoming a near-forgotten starlet. The supporting cast sings excerpts of actual Hokkien operas that she was involved in and gives the musical the background authenticity. Madam Oon narrates her life story including her role playing Titoudao, a witty male servant from a poor background, who is working for a humble kind-hearted scholar, Ti Boon Long. The latter is rejected by his betrothed girlfriend but is helped by her sister, both roles played by male actors. Cross-dressing was a norm for traditional *wayang* productions, and this adds to the humour of the production. When Titoudao's father abandons him and his mother passes away, he is looked after by his mother-in-law who mistreated him. Yet he maintains a cheerful outlook, and remains loyal to his master. The musical is a play within a play in that the opera story parallels present-day real life events of the actors performing the opera. The languages used are Mandarin, Hokkien and Singlish, and they blend seamlessly throughout the production. *Titoudao* was revived several times, and the 2000 revival won the Best Production award at the Life Theatre Awards. It has toured several cities including Cairo, Shanghai, Hangzhou and Beijing, and is now considered a local classic. It also inspired the popular television series Titoudao 2020–2023.

December Rains (1996)

Directed by Goh Boon Teck, *December Rains* was Singapore's second modern-day Chinese-language musical. It was originally staged in 1996. The xinyao music was written by Liang Wern Fook and Jimmy Ye. The story is about a rich girl, Li Qing, who falls in love with her schoolmate Ying Xiong, an idealistic left-wing revolutionary typical of 1950s Singapore. The girl's parents object to their friendship and lock her at home so as to prevent the two communicating with each other. Ying Xiong's idealism drives him to go to China to support the Communist cause and he asks Li Qing to join him. However, she wants Ying Xiong to remain in Singapore and writes him a letter to be delivered by a mutual friend, Ming Li, who has a crush on Li Qing. Ming Li fails to deliver the letter and Ying Xiong sails to China. Thirty years later, Li Qing's daughter, Meng Yu, falls in love with Yang Guang, an actor from China, but Li Qing disapproves of this union, even when she is unaware of Yang Guang's parentage. History is about to repeat itself until Ming Li intervenes and persuades Li Qing to give Yang Guang a chance. When Yang Guang's adoptive parent's fly in to Singapore, Li Qing takes the opportunity to meet them. Yang Guang's adoptive father turns out to be Ying Xiong, the left-wing revolutionary who left Singapore to support the communists in China! Ming Li finally decides to reveal that he was the one who failed to deliver Li Qing's letter to Ying Xiong, but just before he manages to confess, he dies from a heart attack. The xinyao music is pleasant and melodic, but too many sweet ballads fail to capture the emotional highs and lows of the drama. The development of Li Qing and Ying Xiong's love is perhaps too rushed and one does not feel for them. It was restaged in 2010 and 2015.

Mr Beng (1999)

Mr. Beng is a trilingual musical with lyrics and dialogue in Mandarin, Hokkien, and English. The words are written by Otto Fong and music composed by Iskandar Ismail. It was directed by Kok Heng Leun, produced by Drama Box, and staged at the World Trade Centre Auditorium. The story is about Chow Kok Beng, a young contractor, who wants to rid himself of the label "Ah Beng", which stereotypically refers to someone who is disrespected because they are from a low socio-economic class, uncultured, uncouth, and speaks Singlish. Beng falls in love with a rich snooty prig, Peach, who dresses expensively and speaks highfalutin English. Peach tells Beng to abandon his uncultivated friends and adopt a more sophisticated lifestyle embracing fine dining and speaking proper English. He agrees because he wants to rise up the social ladder. Unfortunately, Peach is not in love with Beng, and she is actually out to sabotage him psychologically and financially. Peach has a gay assistant, and when she threatens to expose this assistant's sexual preference to his mother, he sings a powerful painful song revealing that he has now decided to come out of his homosexual closet. The music style has a heavier pulsating western beat with less of the slower lilting xinyao style. Overall *Mr. Beng* is a polished production, with great humour and melodrama, punctuated by excellent dance numbers. The musical explores the clash between Eastern and Western cultures and the grating of the Singapore "caste system". The message conveyed is that one should not be too fixated on socioeconomic status, and instead one should place more value on one's integrity, and to remain true to oneself. It was restaged in 2000.

Lao Jiu (2005)

Another Chinese-language musical is Lao Jiu (2005), which was produced by The Theatre Practice and staged at the Drama Centre. Based on a 1990 play by Kuo Pao Kun, it was adapted into a musical by librettists Zhang Xian and Wu Xi, with dialogue in Mandarin and Hokkien. The lyrics were written by Yang Qian, Wu Xi and Xiao Han, with music composed by Jonathan Price and puppetry by Tan Beng Tian and Rene Ong. The show was directed by Kuo Jian Hong and it was also choreographed by her. The title refers to the ninth and last child, the only son with eight elder sisters born to the Chng family. All the working sisters and their partners have menial jobs, and even the younger sisters who are still schooling are expected to fail their exams. They have a family friend, a traditional Chinese puppeteer, who had earlier predicted before Lao Jiu's birth that he will become highly talented and intelligent. Indeed, his predictions come true and Lao Jiu excels in his studies, and is invited to sit for a scholarship exam that could open the doors to a promising academic or business career. However, he dreams of becoming a traditional puppeteer which was already a dying art form and not likely to earn very much income. In the middle of the exams, Lao Jiu suffers a crisis of confidence and decides to follow his artistic dreams rather than the more bankable career option strongly advocated by his parents and other family members. Lao Jiu has a girlfriend, and the rest of the musical explores their romantic relationship as well as their struggles trying to make ends meet. The musical has a strong storyline and the puppetry is captivating. It was restaged in 2012.

If There're Seasons (2007)

If There're Seasons is a jukebox musical featuring over 30 of Singapore songwriter Liang Wern Fook's popular songs. The songs are in the xinyao Mandarin folk-song style, which Liang Wern Fook started in the 1980s almost single-handedly. The story was written by Hong Kong playwright Raymond To. It was directed by Kuo Jian Hong and Alvin Chiam Hwee Chin, produced by Theatre Practice, and staged in the Drama Centre. The plot follows A-Le, a young Singaporean who moves to New York to start a new life there. He starts work in a Singapore-owned Chinatown pizzeria where he discovers his fellow waiters and deliverymen are all keen on music. So they form a music group to try to earn extra money by entering the music business. In the meantime, A-Le meets Rose, an aspiring actress, and falls in love with her. However, she reminds him of his ex-girlfriend who has earlier passed away, and it affects his relationship with Rose. The outstanding xinyao songs include the title song *If There're Seasons*, *Worry*, and the very sad song *Let's Watch the Sunrise Together*. The production lasted 3 hours, and it is the music that carries the show. It was restaged in 2009 and 2014, and all tickets were sold out.

Liao Zhai Rocks! (2010)

Liao Zhai Rocks! is a Mandarin musical written by Xiaohan and music composed by Eric Ng. It was directed by Kuo Jian Hong and George Chan, produced by The Theatre Practice, and staged at the Drama Centre. Based on a Qing Dynasty classic folk tale, Liao Zhai takes you into a mythical world of fantasy characters. The scholar, Sang Xiao, wins the affections of Ying Ning, a kindly vixen spirit who does not seem to care too much about the scholar. However, Sang Xiao encounters a demon-slayer who is two-faced, and poisons the scholar and throws him into the torturous underworld. It is the vixen spirit Ying Ning who, realising she really loves Sang Xiao, courageously sets out on a dangerous journey to rescue him. The overall tone of the musical is that of a musical comedy, but the opening number is a menacing nightmare scene from hell, which conveys an incongruous feeling difficult to shed. The songs have Chinese-sounding melodies, and they range from magical and spellbinding to loud hard rock genre with a thumping bass. Memorable songs include *Tangled*, and the hummable *Saving My Beloved Life Against Death*. The musical was successfully restaged in 2016.

881 Musical (2011)

In 2011, Goh Boon Teck, the director of Toy Factory Productions, adapted Royston Tan's 2007 film *881* as a musical. Staged at the Esplanade, the

musical tells the story of two friends, Min Min and Yan Yan, who dream of singing in the annual Seventh Month Ghost Festival *getai* stage show. They seek the help of an ex-*getai* singer, Ling, who helps them rehearse and gives them their stage name, 'Papaya Sisters' (which sounds like '881' in Mandarin). Three deities (Fu, Lu and Shou representing happiness, prosperity and longevity) narrate the story and they help the Papaya Sisters, and at the same time they provide slapstick comic relief. Competing for the same *getai* stage are the irritating Durian Sisters from Romania. The Papaya Sisters' prospects end abruptly when Min Min collapses from an undiagnosed brain tumour and eventually dies. *881* is a jukebox musical featuring old Hokkien songs that used to be very popular in their day. Dancing is the weakest element of this musical; the choreography was reviewed as "unadventurous" and the dancers were not well-synchronised. The storyline and songs carry the show, and it has become very successful.

Alkesah (2018)

Alkesah means "as the story goes", and is a Malay language musical written by Zulfadli Rashid and directed by Aidli Mosbit. The music is composed and directed by Elaine Chan, the dances choreographed by Norhaizad Adam and the puppets created by Frankie Malachi Yeo. The main character is Mat Jenin who is an idealistic dreamer and when his father passes away, he inherits the position of village head of Kampung Alkesah. Unfortunately an evil witch Nenek Kebayan has placed a curse on the village resulting

in failing crops and coconut trees dying. The village astrologer tells Mat Jenin that in order to remove the curse he has to brave the difficult climb to the summit of Gunung Saman to meet this witch and do her bidding. En route to the mountain, he meets familiar folklore characters such as the cunning mousedeer Sang Kancil, the intelligent wife Mak Andir and her foolish husband Pak Pandir. Presented in the form of a pantomime the music is melodic and embraces rap dancing. *Alkesah* is a folktale that has an underlying message, asking such questions as who is ultimately responsible for the well-being of a community: a good leader or the members of that community? It injects humour when it suggests that climate change might give an alternative explanation for the village dying plants, and it also explores why truths originating from women is easier to swallow when one hears it coming from male lips. This is an outstanding musical and it won the Best Ensemble award at The Straits Times' Life Theatre Awards 2018.

Quest: The White Hare (2023)

Produced by Toy Factory, *Quest: The White Hare* is a modernisation of an old Hokkien opera for a contemporary audience. The classic tale is about a mysterious white hare who reunites a mother and son after 16 years of separation. To update it, writer and director Goh Boon Teck adds an outer layer where a group of amateur actors are rehearsing the production of this Chinese opera in order to raise money to pay for the company's debts. The contemporary actors speak in Mandarin, Hokkien, and a smattering of Singlish. They are quite humorous and crack jokes alluding to modern-day issues in Singapore contrasting with traditional ideologies. In *Quest: The White Hare*, the opera director is portrayed as extremely dictatorial, harshly admonishing everyone telling them that they are not up to standard. On the opening night, Madame Gwee, the elderly famous star performer inexplicably fails to show up, and at the last moment a young supporting cast member has to quickly stand in for this principal role. A White Hare, played by 7-year-old Asher Kang, appears and unites the mother, Madame Gwee, to her long-lost son Ni Shan. There is a twist at the end when it turns out that the Madame Gwee of the show is an imposter, and the real Madame Gwee shows up at the curtain call to apologise for not being able to perform in the show. The show is well directed by Goh Boon Teck and the tuneful music composed by August Lum reflects the Chinese opera idiom and at the same time appeals to contemporary musical theatre audiences. The producer is Justin Wong, the Chinese opera costumes beautifully designed by Max Tan. The importance of this original creation is that it brings Chinese opera to a modern audience, and this experimentation with the fusion of Chinese opera with Western musical theatre helps in the evolution of an ancient art form into the 21st century.

The Soldier and His Virtuous Wife (2023)

The Soldier and his Virtuous Wife is a modern adaptation of a 2000-year-old Chinese story which has been performed in the past as a Chinese opera. Kuo Jian Hong first produced this musical 30 years ago, but has modernised the current version so it fuses Chinese opera music with that of Western rock music. The playwright and lyricist is Lo Pei-An, the music composed by the late Chen Yang, and the music director and arranger is August Lum, the choreographer Seong Hui Xuan. The story centres around the soldier

Qiu Hu who has just gotten married to Mei Ying when the very next day he is conscripted into the army and sent away to battle. Mei Ying is left behind and is very lonely, but she remains faithful to her husband and spends her days weaving and waiting for his safe return. The original story is tragic in that Mei Ying's virtue is compromised by a rich businessman and she drowns herself in the river. The current Singapore version follows the Yuan Dynasty's happier version when she is reunited with her husband a decade after being separated. Her husband Qiu Hu makes one misstep when he sees a beautiful lady and offers her some gold if she spends a night with him. The lady refuses the offer, and it is only when the soldier returns home that they both recognise each other. The wife is angry that her husband has wanted a one-night stand with her while she has totally refused to indulge in such activity. Now she wants a divorce. It is only when the rich businessman tries to seduce Mei Ying again but this time he is stopped by Qiu Hu that the parents persuade Mei Ying to forgive Qiu Hu and she only does so when he shows more sincerity in his apology. The script is well-written and sparkling humour is sprinkled throughout. The songs are a blend of Chinese opera with Western musical theatre and pop songs. For example, one of the songs starts off with the Abba hit "Money, money, money" before transforming into a more oriental melody and instruments. Another song borrows a snatch of Der Hölle Rache taken from Mozart's The Magic Flute, which adds jocularity to the song. The singing acting and dancing are of the highest standard. The incorporation of Western rhythms to Chinese opera melodies with the addition of some traditional instruments allows the younger audience to appreciate an ancient artform. Singapore sits at the cross-roads between east and west, and the audience appreciates this synthesis of different cultures. This musical demonstrates the evolution of Chinese opera that can capture a modern audience.

Ignite the Sun (2023)

Produced by Goh Boon Teck of Toy Factory in collaboration with the Singapore Chinese Cultural Centre, *Ignite the Sun* is a Chinese-language musical that explores the history of Nanyang Technological University (NTU). The book was written by Quek Yee Kiat, the music composed by Zhang Fan and Elaine Chan who was also the music director. Originally named Nanyang University (Nantah), it was established as a Chinese-medium university by the Chinese-educated community in Singapore, with the goal of providing higher education opportunities for Chinese-speaking students who faced discrimination in English-medium institutions. It was started in 1955 with donations from the Chinese community and also from the entrepreneur Tan Lark Sye. However in the late 1960s and early 1970s, Nantah was beset by student protests and unrest, largely fueled by ideological differences and tensions between the university's leftist student activists and the conservative university administration. The unrest escalated in the 1970s with massive student demonstrations and faculty members demanding the resignation of the university's chancellor. The government response was the closure of Nantah in 1980, and merged it with the University of Singapore to form the new National University of Singapore (NUS). The merger was controversial and faced opposition from some members of the Chinese-educated community, who saw it as a loss of their cultural heritage and identity. The musical tackles all these political issues through stirring and reflective songs, and it softens the political controversy by diverting one's attention by looking at the beauty of the campus where there is a lake that people can fish, and an arch bearing the name and the year Nantah was founded. What carries the musical are the tuneful songs well delivered by the four main singers who represent the students of the university from different time periods of its history. The musical *Ignite the Sun* is an important historical documentation of Nanyang Technological University.

Who Says it First (2023)

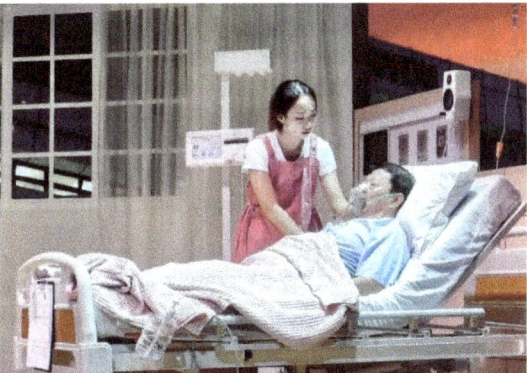

Who Says it First is a Chinese musical with dialogue in Teochew, Mandarin and English. It is produced by Nam Hwa Opera, directed by Jet Ho, with music composed, arranged and directed by Jeff Hue, and lyrics by June Lim, and the book written by Karen Tan. The title song *Who Says it First* is composed by Edmund Ng with lyrics by Lee Jia Min. The lighting and back projection is by Tai Ze Feng. This musical uses Mandopop music with some elements of Chinese music such as the use of a bamboo clapper. It opens with a group of Chinese opera performers entering the room of a Singapore flat dressed in full xifu costume. The story follows Selina, a teenage female student whose behaviour and beliefs are at odds with her elderly grandfather Ah Gong. The opening song, *Here Me Speak* depicts this conflict, when the grandfather sings in Teochew while Selina replies in a mixture of Mandarin and English. They quarrel about many things, including what the program they want to watch on TV, the grandfather's preference for Teochew opera, and his dislike of the clothes worn by young people. But the most pivotal clash is Ah Gong's discovery of Selina's inability to speak and understand Teochew which he blames on her mother's (his daughter Ah Juan) failure to teach her the dialect because she is too busy with her job. This leads to a row between grandfather and granddaughter, then later, when his daughter returns from work, a quarrel between Ah Juan and Selina. The other main element explored in this musical occurs when Ah Gong loses his way and cannot find the restaurant where his family is waiting for him, and we realise that he suffers from dementia. He meets up with his imaginary younger self and collapses on the street. The next scene shows him at a police station where he mistakes his daughter and granddaughter. Later he has further blackouts at home requiring a couple of hospital admissions where initially they think he has a simple stroke, but later we learn that he has an inoperable brain tumour. Humour is injected in several places, including the use of Singapore English (Singlish) especially by Selina's boyfriend who incidentally speaks Hokkien, and later when the Filipino nurse looking after Ah Gong is portrayed as a bit egotistical. The final topic handled by this musical is how one manages the passing on of a loved one. It ends with Selina going to the Teochew opera company to learn how to perform in this art form. The music is lively and melodic, the singing and acting are first-rate and the background projected scenery are most engrossing. This musical is an important Singapore musical because it uses Mandopop music with a hint of Chinese opera, and it deals with important Singapore issues, including the declining use of dialects leading to poorer communication with the elderly, and loss of one's cultural identity. It also highlights the problems with the elderly such as dementia and illnesses, and how a family copes with the loss of a loved one. *Who Says it First* is a landmark Singapore musical.

4 Pantomimes

Introduction

Pantomimes are staged musical productions for children and their families. Originating in England, the shows are usually performed during Christmas and the New Year with an abundance of slapstick humour, gags, and dancing. The storyline typically takes a well-known fairy tale, folk tale or fable and modifies it. The actors often interact with the audience who are encouraged to join in and sing and shout out phrases. In Singapore, pantomimes are also a popular form of end-of-year entertainment with a lot of local humour and a smattering of Singlish incorporated into the production. While retaining the actor-audience interactions, the Singapore pantomime has over the years elevated its standard to incorporate a more moving and deeper philosophical element with a higher standard of book, lyrics and music. Because of this, composer Julian Wong prefers to replace the term "pantomime" with "musical", so as to reflect the elevated level that this art form is currently achieving in Singapore. The major distinction between a musical and a pantomime is that there is greater audience participation in a pantomime. But in Singapore the distinction has become blurred.

The most prominent name in Singapore pantomimes is Ivan Heng and his W!ld Rice Theatre Company. He has produced a show nearly every year towards the end of the year, and it is one of the most popular live theatre shows.

Cinderel-LAH! (2003)

Cinderel-LAH! the pantomime was written by Selena Tan with music by Elaine Chan. It was directed by Ivan Heng, produced by W!ld Rice and staged at the Jubilee Hall of Raffles Hotel. The story is narrated by Ali, the owner of the Mama shop who is married to Jeya, both played by the same person. Poor Cindy lives in a cramped Housing and Development Board (HDB) flat with her evil mahjong-obsessed step-mother and two ugly step-sisters. Prince Char Mee, heir to the world-famous King Crab Restaurant, is holding a Grand Fish Ball where he hopes to choose a bride. Cindy's step-relatives treat her badly, scalding her with hot water, and preventing her going to the ball, singing *You're Nothing But a Maid*. But suddenly, quite by magic, a fairy god Makcik appears, and Cindy is transformed from "no taste" to "fashion ace". She goes to the Fish Ball where she meets Prince Char Mee who immediately falls in love with her, and they sing a beautiful duet *A Waltz to Fall in Love With*. But all is not lost for the ugly step-sisters as they are being pursued by a pair of conjoined twins called Cheng and Heng, which is a spoof of Action Theatre's musical about Siamese conjoined twins Chang and Eng. At midnight, quite predictably, Cindy sprints home leaving one "glass" shoe behind for Prince Char Mee to pick up. The production is very energetic, and the audience participates by cheering the heroes and booing the villains. Overall, it has been a great comedy with unforgettable musical tunes. It was restaged in 2010.

Aladdin (2004)

Written by Selena Tan with music by Elaine Chan, directed by Glen Goei, produced by Ivan Heng's W!ld Rice, *Aladdin* was staged at Jubilee Hall

of Raffles Hotel. Placing it in the Singapore context, Aladdin is a Far East Plaza street teenager who encounters Princess Jasmine, an heiress to Sultan Mustacha from Malacca. However, the pair are unaware of the dangers lurking behind them. The wicked Wizard Abrabanana needs a kid with a pure heart to obtain a magic lamp from the Batu Caves, so he takes Aladdin to the caves. But once Aladdin discovers the magic lamp, he refuses to hand it over to Wizard Abrabanana, who angrily traps the boy inside. Luckily Aladdin accidentally rubs the lamp and a magical genie comes out and grants him his wishes. In the meantime Princess Jasmine's overprotective father locks her up so that she will not marry someone unsuitable. The script is satirical and hilarious, the music has catchy tunes, the dancing is pulsating. A trademark of pantomimes is audience participation, and indeed *Aladdin* has its fair share of cheers and boos. It was restaged in 2011 and the script was rewritten by Jonathan Lim.

Oi! Sleeping Beauty! (2005)

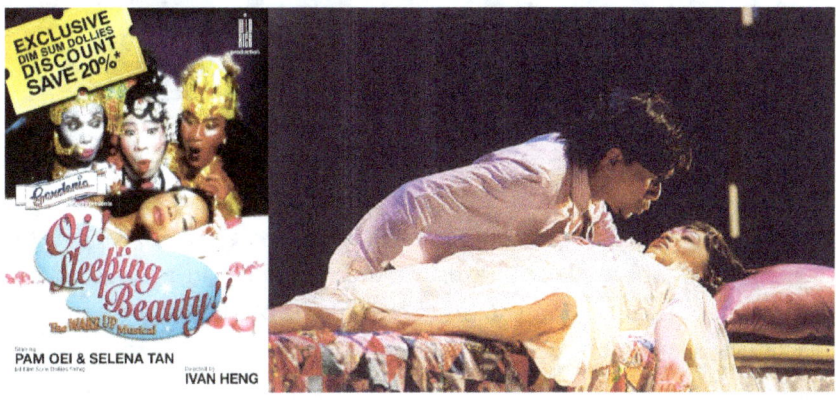

The words of *Oi! Sleeping Beauty!* were written by Jonathan Lim and music composed by Bang Wenfu. Ivan Heng's W!ld Rice produced the show and it was performed at the Drama Centre. Princess Dawn is one month old and her royal family commemorates the Full Month Celebration by having a royal dinner. They invite Fairy Cha Cha Ambo, Fairy Tipah Tertipu, and Fairy Muneru Valliba, representing the three major Singapore Chinese, Malay and Indian communities. But unfortunately the Sultan forgot to invite the evil witch, representing a different ethnic community, who angrily gatecrashes the celebration and places a fatal curse on the princess so when she pricks herself she will die. The three good fairies tried to counter the curse, but the best they can do is to convert it into a sleep that will last 100 years until she gets woken up by a kiss of true love. Indeed, Princess Dawn pricks herself as a teenager and she falls into a deep sleep for a century before she receives a loving kiss from Prince Bin Charming. When she opens her eyes she sees modern Singapore, now known as SingaCorp. The script is full of satirical digs at Singapore, especially with its obsession with the five C's of cash, cars, condos, country club membership and credit cards. All in all, the show is great family fun.

Jack and the Beansprout (2006)

Desmond Sim wrote the book, lyrics by Jonathan Lim and music composed by Elaine Chan. *Jack and the Beansprout* was directed by Jonathan Lim, produced by W!ld Rice and staged at the Drama Centre. To replant the story into Singapore, Jack and his mother are living in a Housing and Development Board (HDB) flat. Strict regulations by HDB restrict the type of animals owners are allowed to keep in the flat, and therefore Jack's mother registers their cow as a dog. The family is hounded by loan sharks who want repayment of their debts. Mother asks Jack to sell their cow to get some money. Now, Jack has been socially isolated because he is attending a "normal" academic stream which in Singapore is a euphemism for being subpar or "lowish" intelligence. Indeed, when Jack tries to sell the cow, he accepts the offer of a handful of beans rather than cash. This infuriates mother who flings the beans out the flat window. Overnight the beans grow to a giant beansprout and Jack decides to climb all the way up. At the top he enters a heavenly palace where he meets a singing harp, a goose that lays golden eggs, and a beautiful blue alien who grabs hold of Jack but becomes attracted to his good looks. Jack also discovers some treasures and steals them to the delight of his mother who is suddenly wealthy and she transforms their poor flat into a lavishly furnished apartment. In the meantime, the owner of the palace is a man-eating giant who is angry that someone is stealing his treasures. When Jack re-enters the palace, he is chased back down the beansprout, whereupon he takes out a chainsaw to cut down the plant. However, the ending has a twist. The message conveyed is that greed and stealing is wrong, and motherly love triumphs. *Jack and the Beansprout* succeeds because it is packed with satirical political humour and risqué jokes and cross-dressing. The sets, costumes, and giant puppets are awesome, and the children swayed to the jaunty songs. The musical was restaged in 2013 with a new book and lyrics by Joel Tan, and new songs added.

Snow White and the Seven Dwarfs (2008)

The book and lyrics of *Snow White and the Seven Dwarfs* was written by Alfian Sa'at and music composed by Elaine Chan. It was directed by Hossan Leong, produced by W!ld Rice and staged in the Drama Centre. Drag Queen is an egomaniac who surrounds her/himself with sycophants. She/he prides her/himself as being the most beautiful person by crowning her/himself the winner of an annual beauty pageant, and this is further confirmed by a magic mirror. But one day the magic mirror informs her/him that she/he is no longer the most beautiful, and discovering that she/he is supplanted by her/his own step-daughter Snow White, the evil Drag Queen arranges cosmetic surgery to uglify the girl. As expected, the plan fails and Snow White looks even more beautiful. The musical is punctuated with subversive socio-political humour, great acting, singing and dancing.

Beauty & the Beast (2009)

Beauty and the Beast was written by Alfian Sa'at and music composed by Elaine Chan. It was directed by Hossan Leong, produced by W!ld Rice and staged at the Drama Centre. The story concerns the family of the merchant Big Boss Bong who has three daughters: two of them, Brandy and Desiree are ugly, while the youngest is named Beauty, and as the name suggests, is beautiful. Looking for a present for Beauty, Big Boss Bong steals a rose from a garden owned by the Beast, but is caught in the act and held captive. His life would only be spared if he promised to bring back one of his daughters. Beauty is brought back to the manor, and she meets a range of characters who work for the Beast, including nanny Ah Ma Chow Chow, cook Baba Pongteh, and maid Vacula Contenssa. In the background is a mysterious exorcist Master Kong who declares he wants to expunge the manor of unnatural elements. Although the Beast falls in love with Beauty, this is not reciprocated because of his ugly looks, but she does feel sorry for him. As with traditional pantomimes, the script is scattered with lewd jokes that the older audience understands but is passed over by the young. One of the songs, *Precious Things* is about saving endangered animals, presumably referring to the Beast. Satirical references to Singaporean idiosyncrasies coupled with lavish sets and costumes, the superb delivery of the triple threat of singing, acting, and dancing, makes this pantomime highly successful.

Hansel and Gretel (2012)

The classical story of *Hansel and Gretel* has been converted into a pantomime with words by Alfian Sa'at and music by Elaine Chan. Directed by Pam Oei and produced by W!ld Rice it was staged at the Drama Centre. The family is living in the Housing and Development Board (HDB) flat in Queenstown, but they are too poor to feed everyone, so the parents ask the two kids to leave home and fend for themselves. They go to the jungles of Mandai, but they are terrified of the glowing eyes and crying sounds in the dark. The next morning, they stumble upon a beautiful cottage with a fence built with fishball sticks with brick walls made of kueh lapis, and roof tiles comprising kaya toast. Hungry, they start devouring the house, but the owner is a crossdressing witch known as "The Chef", who videos herself cooking in a programme called "Makan Mania". She has an assistant called "Nicki Minor" and their antics steal the show. The pantomime is full of satirical barbs and quips. Institutions targeted include the army, national day songs, and even the British royal couple that had recently visited Singapore. Memorable songs include *Irresistible*, *Fighting for Peace* and *In Sunny Queenstown*. Children were given lines to blast the villain, and one goes home satisfied.

Monkey Goes West (2014)

The collaboration of Alfian Sa'at bookwriter and lyricist, with Elaine Chan who composed the music, continues with *Monkey Goes West*. Directed by Sebastian Tan and produced by W!ld Rice, the pantomime was staged at the Drama Centre. Orphan Ah Tang quarrels with his adoptive family and runs away from home. He is transplanted into Haw Par Villa, and has to find his way home in Jurong West. Along the way, he bumps into Monkey King Wukong, warrior Pigsy, crossdressed Princess Iron Fan, loyal river ogre Sandy, Red Boy, and King Bull; they all help him get home. But the journey is surprisingly dangerous, and they will encounter mythical monsters, tricksy fairies and other demons. The script is littered with politically incorrect jokes, and cheeky references to pop culture. The performance showcased young children doing kungfu dances, and the songs ranged from fast-paced toe-tapping to the emotional song of Ah Tang's mother passing on. Audience participation was encouraged. The overall message was successfully conveyed, which is the importance of one's family, and of working together as a team. It was restaged in 2016.

The Emperor's New Clothes (2015)

Hans Christian Andersen's story has been converted into a musical-pantomime by writer Joel Tan, with music composed by Julian Wong, directed by Dim Sum Dolly's Pam Oei and produced by W!ld Rice. The Emperor is a pompous narcissistic megalomaniac and he is enraged when the foreign press reports not on his new clothes he is showing off at his special New Dress Parade (NDP), but rather they write about the lively music instead. He jails the journalists as well as the musicians. He then hires two new tailors to make him superior clothes for his next birthday, but the Emperor does not realise that the two tailors he has chosen are charlatans. They promise him they will weave such a fine set of clothes that the Emperor will not be able to see them; and thereby the tailors will expose, quite literally, the Emperor's egoistic witlessness. The two tailors are dazzling in their ability to act, sing and dance together, and they sing the humorous song *Brother from Another Mother*. The Emperor also sings a catchy song *Naked as My Butt*. The children from W!ld Rice programme for the young are so adorable and nearly steal the whole show. Music is a vital component of musicals, but what is so innovative about this production is that the actors accompany themselves playing their own instruments, eg playing the violin while they sing. This adds another dimension to their talents. The brilliant songs that capture the different moods so perfectly are composed by the internationally acclaimed composer and music director, Julian Wong. The script is full of satirical references to Singapore's past colonial rule, Singapore's Internal Security Department, the Singapore Idol, etc. They even make reference to a television drama serial where the Emperor's wife, Empress Jeanette, tortures a captive audience with her bad singing (an insider joke). The deeper message of this musical is that we need to look at our leaders critically and not to worship the ground they walk on. After all, under their veneer, they are like all of us, naked.

Mama White Snake (2017)

Mama White Snake's book and lyrics were written by Alfian Sa'at with music composed by Elaine Chan. It was directed by Pam Oei, produced by W!ld Rice and staged at the Drama Centre. The story revolves around Meng, who is looked after by his mother and his aunt in the Emei Mountains. But these two ladies, played by crossdressers, do not allow him to leave the mountains, explaining that there is danger lurking outside. Disobedient, Meng leaves home and enrols in a martial arts school run by Master Fahai, where he falls in love with his daughter, Mimi. Fahai wants to reek revenge on Meng's mother and aunt, so he reveals that they are actually the White Snake and Green Snake of mythology. Chaos breaks out, and a small army of young children join the wushu fighting between the clans. Later a herd of kids dressed as baby pandas dance about delightfully. Edgy jokes and great songs make the pantomime enjoyable. And in the end, true love triumphs.

A $ingapore Carol (2018)

Written by Jonathan Lim with music by Elaine Chan, *A $ingapore Carol* was directed by Hossan Leong and presented at the Victoria Theatre. The Charles Dickens story has been translocated to Singapore. The central character is the wealthiest businessman in Singapore, Mr SK Loo. He also happens to be the stingiest and the meanest. He spends all his time planning hostile takeovers and then retrenching all the staff. It opens with Mr SK Loo giving a Teddy Talk on how to make money while ignoring ethics. That night he is visited by three ghosts from the past, present and future. They present him with excerpts of his life. Several innovations were incorporated into the production, including asking the audience to use their mobile phones as a prompt when to cheer or boo, and using special lighting to create a virtual columbarium for the dead with projected flowers. To give an eastern feel, one of the Christmas spirits is a hantu (Malay ghost of the dead), and the future ghost is an avatar of the businessman trying to sell his appstall goods. No pantomime is complete without digs at the problems of contemporary Singapore including addiction to unsocial media causing social isolation. Memorable music includes the dancing song *A Million of Me*, the emotional *Christmas Out There*, and the hummable finale *Christmas No Enough*. Ultimately *A $ingapore Carol* delivers the message of the importance of love and the spirit of giving.

Peter Pan in Serangoon Gardens (2019)

Peter Pan in Serangoon Gardens is difficult to classify. Produced by W!ld Rice that has staged over 10 new pantomimes (with some repeats) since 2003. This latest production has edged towards the classification border between a pantomime and a musical. Some elements of a pantomime are retained, such as audience participation, the comic fairy tale story line with crossdressed characters and provocative jokes. But it has gone upmarket with an insightful book written by Thomas Lim, heartfelt lyrics by Joel Tan, and professional music by Julian Wong. It was impeccably directed by Ivan Heng and staged at W!ld Rice's brand new theatre at Funan Centre complete with quality sets, costumes, lighting, sound system, etc. The DeSouza family living in Serangoon Gardens has 3 children, all struggling with the Singapore pressure cooker educational system. They get a visit from Peter Pan, the boy who never grows up, played by a female who lures them away. Together with his overweight fairy companion, Ting Tong Bell, played by a male, Peter Pan and the three kids fly to Neverland. It is quite incredible to see these actors pretending to fly while they are actually suspended in mid-air. They meet a gang of Lost Boys, and they are all captured by evil Captain Hook and his two side-kicks, Simi and Daichi (in Hokkien the two words together mean "What's Wrong?") The final message conveyed by this musical (yes, this pantomime can be given a "musical" certificate!) is that you must believe everything is possible, even the impossible. Just let your imagination fly!

Momotaro and the Magnificent Peach (2021)

Momotaro and the Magnificent Peach is a pantomime which was performed at the end of 2021, when the COVID-19 pandemic in Singapore was falling. Every day, the cast had to be tested for COVID-19 before the show, the audience had to wear masks and they were socially distanced in their seating, and no food was allowed in the theatre. The show went on. Words were written by Dwayne Lau and music composed by Elaine Chan. It was directed by Glen Goei, produced by W!ld Rice, and staged in their new theatre in Funan Centre. Momotaro, also known as "Momo", is a boy found in a peach by a childless couple. Now he is a teenager living in Peach Paradise, a beautiful unspoilt island. One day, a devastating wave of poisonous pollution surrounds the island and the wildlife starts to die. Momo decides to take up the challenge to save the environment and protect his family, friends and wildlife. He befriends three animal companions, a hunting dog, a crane, and a snow monkey. The villains include a President with a hairstyle that bears resemblance to a former US President, who wants to "Make us great again!" The stage is filled with piles of trash stretching all the way to the front row seats. Momo and his animal friends have to battle the enemy using ancient Japanese swords and spears, and the fight scenes are visually most exciting. Then the friends have to clean up all the garbage. There are clever references to climate change, waste disposal, and the use of "circuit breakers". Memorable songs include the opening number *Welcome to Peach Paradise!*, and the J-Pop style song *Let Me Influence You, Baby*, and Momo singing *Who Am I?* The pantomime covers many socio-political issues, but finally it is about the power of friendship that can defeat evil and solve the planet's problems.

Pinocchio (2022)

W!ld Rice's production of Pinocchio is a wonderfully humorous and simultaneously touching musical. The book was written by Thomas Lim, the music composed by Julian Wong and the lyrics by Joel Tan and directed by Pam Oei. Based on the original story of a woodcutter Geppetto who creates the puppet Pinocchio, and a blue fairy who visits the workshop and gives Pinocchio the ability to walk and talk, but also gives him a nose that will elongate whenever he tells a lie. To achieve the goal of becoming a real flesh-and-blood boy, Pinocchio has to prove that he is brave, true and kind. Helped by a companion insect, a grasshopper named G-Hopper in Wild Rice's version, and not Disney's cricket, Pinocchio is given some money by Geppetto to buy books for school. But he is diverted by a couple of con men, a Cat and a Fox, who cheat him out of his money by persuading Pinocchio to watch a phony circus show. They further lead him to another villain, who transforms children into donkeys and enslaves them. Pinocchio and G-Hopper manage to escape from this rogue only to be swallowed up by a giant whale. By chance they meet up with Geppetto who was also swallowed up by the same whale while searching for Pinocchio. To escape from the whale, they tickle its throat and when it sneezes, they are expelled. Geppetto suffers from near-drowning and is saved by Pinocchio, who unfortunately becomes lifeless. However, his selfless sacrifice earns Pinocchio a final magic wish from the blue fairy, and he is transformed into a real boy. At this point the audience and the author wept with tears of joy. This is the power of W!ld Rice's reincarnation of Pinocchio the musical. Every aspect worked, from the hummable songs to the strong characterisations, the dancing, the set design, and the projected images. One must mention the six young children in the supporting cast who made the show so engaging: they are the heart of the musical.

Reference

1. Alfian Sa'at. Twenty Years of W!ld Rice (2023). Epigram Books. ISBN: 9789814845885

Websites Archives

1. Centre42 Archives: https://www.centre42.sg/
2. W!ld Rice Archives: https://www.wildrice.com.sg/
3. TheatreWorks Past Productions: https://theatreworks.org.sg/cover/home.htm
4. Singapore Repertory Theatre Past Productions: https://www.srt.com.sg/past-productions-and-licensing
5. Musical Theatre Ltd Past Productions: https://mtlmanager.wixsite.com/mtl5/our-history

5 Operas

Introduction

Although operas are not conventionally classified as musicals, the boundary between these two genres is sometimes blurred. Operas are generally sung through with very little spoken dialogue, although even some famous operas like *Carmen* and *Fidelio* contain unsung spoken lines. Then there are musicals that are sung-through with virtually no spoken dialogue, like *Cats*, *Les Misérables*, *Phantom of the Opera*, and *Hamilton*. These musicals with hardly any spoken words are considered a form of modern opera by some.

What are the other distinguishing features between an opera and a musical? Opera performers may only have one or two of the triple threats (dancing, acting and singing), in contrast to what most musical theatre performers possess. Opera singers usually have a more powerful voice enriched by vibrato. In previous centuries, before the invention of amplifying microphones, opera singers had to project their voices by singing loudly. However, in recent years, there have been increasing number of operas performed (especially in Singapore) where the singers amplify their voices electronically.

Perhaps the major difference between an opera and a musical is that in operas, music is the driving force, whereas in musicals, words are the prime movers. The style of music in operas leans towards a more orchestral classical style and tends to avoid the heavy rhythmic drumbeats. Operas are not that popular in Singapore, as judged by the audience sizes and revenues generated by their performances, and hence there are relatively few original operas written compared to musicals.

Singapore is slowly venturing into the operatic domain. The first opera written and performed is Bunga Mawar (1997) with music composed by the late Matthew Leong Yoon Pin, and libretto written by Edwin Thumboo. In recent years there has been a slow but steady stream of new operas being written and staged in Singapore. Currently an up-and-coming opera composer making a mark is Chen Zhangyi of the Yong Siew Toh Conservatory of the National University of Singapore. Music critic Chang Tou Liang said of Zhangyi: "Chen should no longer be referred to as a composer of promise, but one of stature."

Bunga Mawar (1997)

Bunga Mawar (The Rose) is Singapore's first original opera and was premiered in 1997. The English libretto was written by Edwin Thumboo and music composed by Matthew Leong Yoon Pin. The project was initiated by Choo Hwee Lim, who invited Leong Yoon Pin to write the music. Later, he founded Singapore Lyric Theatre together with Leow Siak Fah. The opera was directed by Hugh Halliday and the orchestra was conducted by Lim Yau. "Bunga Mawar" translates into "The Rose." The main story revolves around Andre Wong and his wife-to-be, Charlotte Tan. Andre works for his father whose wealth comes from property, finance and transport, while Charlotte is a business lady and she is of Peranakan heritage. The opera is a love story and opens and closes with a Peranakan wedding pageant. The music is halfway between lyrical and dissonant. The libretto contains recitatives, poetic soliloquies, duets and pantun which is a Malayan poetic form of Peranakan culture. For Singapore's first opera, this is a good attempt to forge a Singapore identity.

Fences (2012)

Fences is the second Singapore opera and was the brainchild of Leow Siak Fah. The libretto was written by Robert Yeo and the music composed by John Sharpley and they have been working on it for eight years before it was finally staged by Opera Viva at the Lee Foundation Theatre in the Nanyang Academy of Fine Arts. It is a love story between Malay Nora Ibrahim from Malaya and a Chinese Singaporean Steven Lee who meet in Malaya Hall in London in the 1960s. When they return home and inform their parents, both encounter objections to their relationships by their respective parents. Earlier Nora teases Steven with *You Have Waiting in Your Eyes*, and when they face problems with their families, they sing *What is This Stench Called Race?* and *What Coming Home Means*. At that time, Singapore was still part of Malaysia, but when racial riots erupted, the Malaysians were unhappy with Singapore, as expressed in the song *Crush Lee Kuan Yew!* In 1965, when Singapore is expelled from Malaysia, the Singapore prime minister sings an indignant defiant song. The two families erect a metaphorical fence that divides them. Will true love break through the racial and religious fences? Overall the music is melodious and romantic, and beautifully orchestrated with the addition of marimba, pantun and gamelan for the Malay family scenes, and the use of the erhu, yangqin and dizi for the Chinese family scenes. The singing is of international standard.

Pursuant (2013)

Pursuant is a musical-opera produced by Singapore's Lyric Opera. Music was composed by Chen Zhangyi and the libretto written by Jonathan Lim. It was staged at the Drama Centre. Set in a futuristic dystopic state of Singacorp, the story revolves around Ethan, a teenage boy who is arrested by the thought police for harbouring dreams. In this nation, dreaming has been banned because it prevents the citizens from achieving perfect productivity. At his trial, the judge interrogates Ethan's parents and while they are unaware of their son's dreaming, they acquiesce to his sentencing into a CC (Concentration Camp). There Ethan meets other youths also found guilty of dreaming, and were sent for correction at this camp. In particular he meets a girl, Shufang, who is a Cosplay (video game of dressing up characters) fanatic, and Terry who has ADHD (Advanced Dream Hyperactivity Disorder). With the help of an underground rebel organization the children manage to escape from the camp. In the meantime Ethan tells of his recurrent dream of an Old Man whose picture looks suspiciously like Lee Kuan Yew, Singapore's founding father. The Old Man's dreams have laid the foundation for creating his nation, but because he wants the nation to adopt his dreams only, he bans other from dreaming. The political satire is obvious. Only when the Old Man has a heart attack and undergoes a change of heart, that he allows Ethan and others to dream on. The score is operatic in feel but has a modern style. There is sufficient variety and energy to make the music quite appealing. The singers are well supported by the orchestra conducted by composer Chen Zhangyi. This musical sits between humorous spoof and serious propaganda. The parody of Singapore life and politics is laugh-out-loud funny. The jingoistic anthem-like songs towards the end are a bit out of keeping with the overall cheeky irreverent tone of the rest of the musical. *Pursuant* is a highly original work and it is a bold attempt to introduce satire and modern music into Singapore opera.

A Singapore Trilogy (2012–2018)

Artwork by Alvin Mark Tan

A Singapore Trilogy is an assembly of three separate chamber operas: (a) *Laksa Cantata* (2012, 2018), (b) *Window Shopping* (2014), and (c) *Kopi For One* (2018), with music by Chen Zhangyi and libretto by Jack Lin. It was directed by Nora Samosir and staged at The Arts House, Singapore. It was produced by L'arietta Productions in 2020 during the COVID-19 pandemic where it was part of the "30 days of Art Festival."

(a) **Laksa Cantata** (2012, 2017)
Laksa Cantata is a one-act chamber opera with music by Chen Zhangyi and libretto written by Jack Lin. At the beginning of the opera, Stephen is counting down to his forthcoming wedding. His fiancée Leah, enters and scolds him for his outrageous idea of serving laksa at their wedding banquet! He 'faces the music' with Leah's aria *A Woman's Scorned*, where she vents her frustrations and they quarrel. In the *Laksa Aria*, Stephen confesses his

ardent love of laksa and his adamant intention to retain it at the banquet. Leah tries to win the argument by threatening to have his future-mother-in-law stay with them in their new apartment. In an attempt to resolve the tension, they launch into a duet *Agree to Disagree*, and they end with a finale duet *A New Bowl is A New Day*, where they reconcile and celebrate their bright future ahead in matrimony. This opera is amusing to watch.

(b) **Window Shopping** (2014)

Window Shopping is a one-act chamber opera with music by Chen Zhangyi and libretto by Jack Lin. It is about a woman and a young bright-eyed girl. Set in a shoe shop, each character explores the personal relationship one has with oneself, and how each person develops over time. The woman is in her thirties, and she wanders into the shoe shop, taking her time to browse through the shop with a sense of nostalgia while she reminisces about her visit to the same store many years ago. Each pair of heels in the shoe boutique reminds her of her past, and she laments to herself about memories of her youthful folly. A girl enters the shop full of excitement and announces that it is *Time to Shop!* As if on a shopping spree, she portrays herself as a carefree shopaholic in *Shopping Aria*. The woman and the girl seem unaware of each other's presence, as they browse through the shop, and they both arrive at the same blue pair of shoes with special heels that have both women transfixed; one is teeming with excitement, while the other is overwhelmed by memories. The woman laments about her past in self-reflection, while the girl looks forward to her unknown but hopefully bright future, where *'each sole (soul) has a new story to tell'*. The opera concludes open-endedly, without either character making any purchase.

(c) **Kopi for One** (2018)

In this final instalment of the trilogy, the opera opens to a ubiquitous kopitiam (Singaporean coffeeshop) where a waitress is seen cleaning and sweeping the floor. She complains about her life and work. It is evident that the waitress has been working for many years at the kopitiam, and she has become somewhat jaded and weary of her customers and her daily chores. Soon a younger woman enters the premises and is instantly recognized by the waitress. The two catch up over some small talk, and she eventually orders herself a coffee. Later, an elderly man enters, and is greeted by the waitress as an old friend and customer. The old man has come to the kopitiam to try to reconcile with her daughter, the younger woman. The waitress understands this predicament and leaves to give the family some space. The father and daughter have an indirect conversation, and a commotion ensues, which leaves the daughter in tears and her father leaving the kopitiam. As he leaves, he tries to convey his final affection to her but visibly fails to move her. The waitress re-enters with their drinks and notices that the father has left, and the daughter is in an emotional state. She tries to console her, asking what the quarrel was about. After composing herself, the daughter is perplexed by the question and responds that she has been the only customer in the kopitiam the entire time. The opera ends with a moment of confoundment as we find out the daughter had just attended her father's funeral service before coming to the kopitiam.

Panic Love (2020)

Panic Love is an a capella opera written and filmed during the COVID-19 pandemic. The libretto was authored by Felix Cheong, and music composed by Chen Zhangyi, directed by dramaturg/director Nora Samosir and film director Lim Ziyu. During the COVID-19 pandemic, flights are grounded, so air stewardess Mariam loses her job and becomes a social distancing enforcer, a role she takes on overzealously. At the height of the pandemic the Ministry of Health introduces harsh "circuit breaker rules" forcing people to distance from each other and not allowing them to sit in food courts or restaurants. An elderly man is sitting alone having a drink in a hawker stall and when Mariam sees him, she issues him a fine for breaking the rules. Unfortunately when her mother is dying in a nursing home, Mariam learns that she is not allowed to visit her. It is ironic that the rules she enforces on others is being enforced on her. Three guys sing the acapella accompaniment and provide light relief. As theatres and cinemas were closed during this period, *Panic Love* was not staged in a theatre but filmed and broadcast as a video. The opera questions how strictly one needs to enforce regulations and what degree of flexibility is allowed when it is a matter of life and death.

Kampung Spirit (2021)

This is an opera in two episodes with music by Chen Zhangyi and libretto by Sara Florian. Set in the 1970s, *Kampung Spirit* is about an imaginary kampung in Singapore, inspired by Liu Kang's iconic oil canvas painting "Life by the River" (1975), displayed at the National Gallery, Singapore. Through the fantasy of magic realism, a timeless Narrator makes the characters come to life. These characters relive the bygone days of a simple kampung life that intertwined so closely with nature, by the riverside. The theme of 'water' starts and ends the opera, acting as a cathartic, unifying vector. Through the Narrator's interwoven stories of the characters, who come to life as in *a tableau vivant*, one can perceive an Arcadian sense of nostalgia, but also a sense of hope for the future. Musically, the "New Nanyang Style" of composition paints the contrasts between the urgent rhythms and leisurely charm of these kampung characters, and pays homage to the colourful and bold brushstrokes of Liu Kang's painting style.

Inconvenience of Minor Parts (2021)

Inconvenience of Minor Parts is an opera with music composed by Hoh Chung Shih and the libretto by Felix Cheong. It was staged at the Esplanade Concourse in 2021. The scene is contemporary and is about an ageing television actress who is preparing for an interview about to happen. She looks back at her life with sadness and the sacrifices she has made for her daughter over the past 30 years. In her early days she was popular and successfully secured lead roles. But as she got older, she can only scrape for minor roles. The opera is a bitter look at how the youth are worshipped in society, while the elderly are neglected.

Arianna On Another Island (2022)

Watercolour by Sara Florian

Arianna on Another Island is a children's opera with music composed by Chen Zhangyi, and the libretto written by Sara Florian. The story is about Arianna, a little girl from Singapore who is listening to her father telling a bedtime story about the Greek myth of Ariadne. In her imaginary dream-journey, she travels around Singapore pretending to be the mythological heroine. She visits Sentosa, the Bird Park, the zoo, the Aquarium, the Botanic Gardens and the River Safari, until she reaches the harbour at Marina Bay Sands, and she learns something really important about the relationship between humans and Mother Nature from a chorus of Mermaids and from Bacchus himself. Children really enjoy this opera.

The Butterfly Lovers (2023)

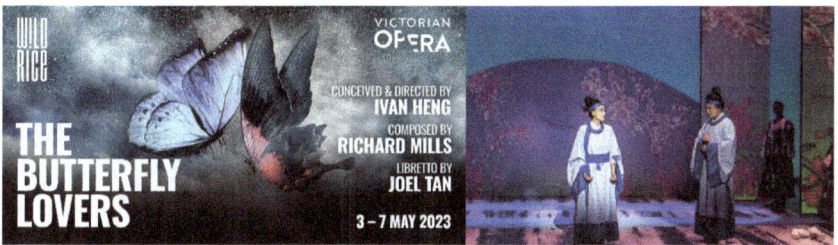

Conceived and directed by Ivan Heng, and jointly produced by W!ld Rice and Australia's Victoria Opera The Butterfly Lovers has music composed by Richard Mills and a libretto written in English by Joel Tan. It is aptly staged in Singapore's Victoria Theatre. The story is taken from an ancient Chinese Eastern Jin Dynasty (266–420 AD) legend, during a time when females did not get support for higher education. The heroine, Zhu Yingtai has managed to persuade her father to send her to the academy, but she has to disguise herself as a man to study there. En route to the academy she meets Liang Shanbo, and they discover they are going to the same establishment. On arrival they find that they have to share the same room that only has one double bed. They hide their romantic feelings for each other because of the social conventions of the time, but while sleeping together Shanbo unconsciously puts his arms around Yingtai. The teaching master knows Zhu Yingtai's family and when Yingtai tells him that there are two brothers, he checks and discovers that the family has one son and one daughter. He confronts Yingtai and reveals he knows that she is female, but will allow her to remain in his class. In the meantime, Yingtai's father has received an offer from a wealthy businessman to marry his daughter. He agrees and sends a messenger calling Yingtai to return home immediately. Shanbo accompanies Yingtai for part of her journey home, and initially he stops halfway. But later he decides to go to Yintai's home, and to his surprise he is met by a lady, who claims to be Yingtai's sister. Shanbo soon realises that she is indeed his classmate and tries unsuccessfully to persuade Yingtai to return with him to the academy. He is devastated when he learns that she is engaged to be married. Heartbroken Shanbo travels back, but falls seriously ill and dies. Yingtai is forced by her father to marry the wealthy businessman, and en route to be married, she sees the grave stone of Shanbo with his clothing next to it. Immediately she wants to join Shanbo, and forces the grave to open up. Their spirits emerge and the two ascend into heaven, happily united. The singing is powerful and the emotions are very moving. Yingtai's role is sung by an actress with a beautiful soprano voice and is also convincing in her role. Shanbo is played by a countertenor, which is a brilliant tactic because his voice can easily be mistaken for a female's. It retains the same sex implication of these two characters. Richard Mills is to be congratulated for his wonderful music and orchestration, with the addition of pipa and dizi to give it a Chinese feel. The production is an outstanding fusion of eastern and western art forms.

References

1. Singapore Trilogy
   Video: https://www.youtube.com/watch?v=cF1TtLSkq6E
2. Laksa Cantata
   Complete video: https://www.youtube.com/watch?v=7bysWX9xXWQ
3. Window Shopping
   Complete Video: https://www.youtube.com/watch?v=D3kNDTq-bLk
   Trailer: https://www.youtube.com/watch?v=XimT--2BsMl
4. Kopi for One
   Synopsis: https://www.chenzhangyi.com/kopi-for-one

5. Panic Love video: https://www.youtube.com/watch?v=wIdvV3axIEA&t=543s
6. Kampong Spirit
   Synopsis from https://www.chenzhangyi.com/kampungspirit
   Video: https://www.facebook.com/NACSingapore/videos/656620605366421/
7. Inconvenience of Minor Parts:
   https://www.youtube.com/watch?v=eFQDnkP3UBA
8. Arianna on Another Island
   Synopsis: https://www.chenzhangyi.com/arianna-on-another-island
9. The Butterfly Lovers review: https://www.straitstimes.com/life/arts/wild-rice-and-victorian-opera-give-the-butterfly-lovers-a-sexy-retelling

6 School and University Campus Musicals

Introduction

There are a fairly large number of musicals written by Singapore students attending educational institutions, ranging from secondary schools, junior colleges, polytechnics and universities. What campus musicals excel in is their creativity. Ideas range from modifying existing stories in imaginative ways, to creating new universes for the characters to live in. The script, lyrics, music, choreography, costume and set designs are entirely new. In recent years, an increasing number of Singapore schools and tertiary institutions have written and staged original musicals. The musicals selected for inclusion in this chapter are those largely written or produced by students, and are performed entirely by students. The stories school musicals tell reflect Singapore's educational system as well as the current views of a younger generation on ethical and other issues. Campus musicals spark creative playwriting, music composition, choreography, set and costume designs, plus they encourage teamwork. Historically it is well-known that most famous creative teams in Broadway and West End musicals started off during their student days. This holds true for Singapore as well, and therefore it is a tradition that should be cultivated for the future of Singapore theatre. This chapter features selected musicals that the author has been involved in and watched.

Song of the Whale (2001)

Song of the Whale is a musical based on the story from the Book of Jonah, where Jonah is running away from his duty to help the citizens of Ninevah.

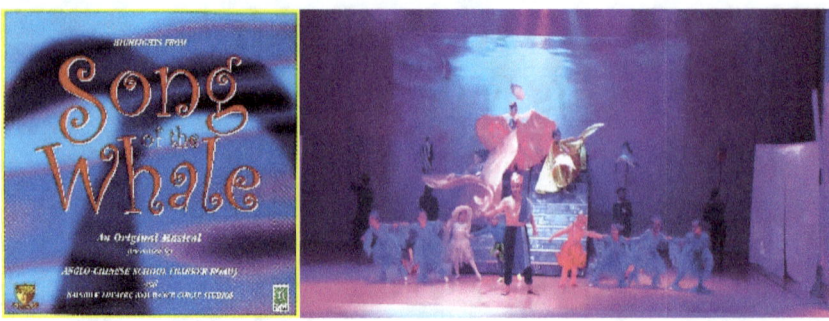

But during his sea voyage, a storm arises and the sailors have to throw him into the sea in order to quell the storm. Luckily Jonah is rescued by being swallowed into a whale. The book and lyrics were written by Sean Cheong and music composed by Joshua Chua, both students of Anglo-Chinese School (ACS) where the musical was staged. Additional lyrics were written by Hoang Du'c, and additional songs were written by Kenneth Lyen. All the cast members were students from ACS. Memorable songs include the title number *Song of the Whale*, and *To Sea*. The performance was very energetic with lively dancing and the storm scene was quite realistic. The musical was restaged in Jakarta in 2020.

Exodus (2003)

The musical *Exodus* was composed by ACS student Joshua Chua Yao Zhang, and additional songs by Kenneth Lyen. The book and lyrics were

written by Stella Kon, and the entire cast were students from the primary and secondary schools. Based on the biblical chronicles, the plot is focused on the conflict between Moses and Pharaoh. Moses is determined to free the Israelites and he inflicts ten plagues on Egypt, and on the death of Pharaoh's son, they are set free. However, Pharaoh changes his mind and pursues the Israelites but when crossing the Red Sea, his army is drowned. The musical consists of hummable tunes in several songs: *Lead Me I'll Follow*, *Lamb Little Lamb*, and *Go Moses Go*. The finale *To the Promised Land* is a rousing number that had the whole audience clapping along. The musical was restaged in 2018 in Jakarta.

Making the Grade (2004)

The book and lyrics were written by Ng Swee San, and the music composed by Karen Lim and Kenneth Lyen. The entire cast, orchestra, backstage administration, ticket sales and other production matters were managed by the students of Methodist Girls' School, with an age range from 7 to 16 years. The two main characters are teenage schoolgirl Anita and her new teacher, Mei. Anita's mother is poorly educated and is working in the school as a cleaning lady. This is embarrassing for Anita, so she gets angry when mother gives her a cheap birthday present. Her classmates and Anita run into trouble when they skip class to welcome an overseas pop group. But their absence from Mei's class leads to their being reported and sent to detention. We learn that teacher Mei is being offered an overseas scholarship provided she confirms that she is free during that entire period. However, she is committed to looking after her disabled sister with Down Syndrome. She lies to the headmistress, hiding the fact that she cannot leave her sister who requires a great deal of care. The music ranges from poignant lyrical to robust dance numbers. The school orchestra provides sensitive and strong backing.

Roulette (2012)

The script of *Roulette* was written by university students from Raffles Hall, National University of Singapore (NUS) Hoon Ding Yi, Yvonne Alain Lek, The Huiying, and it based on *Casino*, an original musical by Kenneth Lyen and Richard Lord. Additional songs were by Klaus Kristian, also a university student. *Roulette* was staged at the University Cultural Centre. Set in Golden Sands, a fictitious casino, the story centres around Everett, an innocent 21-year-old university student, who has just come of age, and is legally allowed to visit the casino for the very first time in his life. He is being mentored by two senior employees of the casino, Morgen Stanley Tan and Vera Stearns. Unknown to him, these two veterans are using him to ensnare a benevolent Robin Hood who is depriving the casino of its earnings by consistently winning, and then giving his takings to unfortunate gamblers who have lost all their money. We learn the reason why

Everett wants to make a lot of money when he takes a toilet break, and it is because he wants to win back his girlfriend who has just ditched him because of his lack of money. Everett makes a killing at all the different tables, earning a lot of money. Everett then puts all his winnings into a roulette game and although he guesses the right number, the casino staff informs him that the rules do not allow him to take the money. The acting was excellent the well-synchronised dancing lifted the performance to a very high standard. The cast and crew was incredibly large, and over 200 people were involved in this production.

Firefly in the Light (2014)

The book, music and lyrics of *Firefly in the Light* were written by Shayna Toh of Raffles Institution, who also produced the musical. The story is about teenager Wendy who is searching for something to fill the emptiness in her life. Torn between a possessive mother, her childhood sweetheart Jake, and vivacious friends, Wendy leaves home in search of city lights, fame, and a long-lost father. Seven years later, Wendy and Jake's destinies cross once again. With the rekindling of love within her grasp, Wendy must first find her own inner calling, and she has to decide whether to pursue stardom or to settle for love. But complicating matters is the uncovering of a dark family secret. *Firefly in the Light* is a pop-rock musical about ambition, loyalty, and truth of identity. The musical was restaged in 2017 at the New York Musical Festival, and again in 2019 at Brown University.

Atlas Unbound (2014)

The National University of Singapore Medical Society created the original musical *Atlas Unbound* which was staged at Kallang Theatre. Everyone involved, from the creative and performing teams were all medical students. The music was composed and directed by Chu Ben Wee and was avant garde semi-classical semi-operatic in style. The hero follows instructions by his dying father to go on a quest that will honor their family. The problem of the musical is that the purpose of the travel is not revealed, and although the hero encounters mystical spirits, makes friends, and is also betrayed by some, and there is some romance and love in a foreign land, the musical ends without a resolution. For a student musical each individual component of the musical: the book, the songs, and the choreography were excellent, but the story line was difficult to follow.

Keep the Flame (2015, 2023)

Keep the Flame is a musical written by Brian Seward with music by Karen Lim, and performed by the primary school children ages from 7 to 13 years old, all attending St Andrew's Junior School. Set in the distant future where the planet earth is burnt dry and everything is dying. Three volunteers are sent back in time to the year 2199 to find out why humans were exploiting the earth and each other for their own selfish greed. The time travelers are being followed by two minions sent by their boss, Professor Evil, who is responsible for the earth's disaster. Accidentally landing at several wrong time zones, they make it to 1954 during the devastating Singapore floods. The two minions are drowning and are rescued by the three volunteers, whereupon they become friends. They travel together to 2199 hoping to prevent a young schoolboy who is about to turn villainous. They learn that the reason this schoolboy is turning bad is because he is being bullied by his classmates. Luckily, they are able to rewind the clock to prevent the bullying and thereby avert the creation of Professor Evil. The musical ends with the song *Let the Flame Burn Brighter*. The production celebrates the 153rd anniversary of the school, and the story incorporates its history when in 1862 the Anglican Church adopted a struggling local school and renamed it St Andrew's. The musical is very moving and brought tears of joy to the audience.

Viva Lah Singapura! (2015)

Written and produced by students of Raffles Hall, National University of Singapore, *Viva Lah! Singapura* was staged at the University Cultural Centre of the National University of Singapore. The book writer was Sebastian Ang and the composer was Jonathan Shin, and both took part in writing the lyrics. The musical revolves around Happy Laksa House, which is being acquired by a multimillionaire property developer after the death of the founder, Ah Hock's father. Ah Hock inherited the restaurant and became the sole chef. He has a daughter, Rachel, but is unable to see eye-to-eye with her, in part because he objects to her ambitions to embrace music as her career. While singing at a bar, Rachel is noticed by Darren, who is attracted to her. He recognizes her as Ah Hock's daughter because he has seen them at Happy Laksa House which he frequents. Darren is disillusioned with his current office job and secretly wants to become a laksa chef, so he approaches Rachel. There are gentle pokes at the difficulties of doing business in Singapore, and the compulsory military service for boys. Whenever the social network service Twitter is spoken, you hear the sounds of tweeting birds, and highly exaggerated embellishment of the word "hashtag" adds to the jocularity. The songs are humorous and there are gentle digs at Singapore's propensity to use acronyms in the song *Home is No ABC*. Catchy lyrics are also found in such songs such as: *Happy Laksa House*, *Why? Why? Why? Why?*, and *Stars*. Overall, a high standard was displayed in *Viva Lah Singapura!*

The Girl with the Red Balloon (2016)

Raffles Hall, National University of Singapore's students wrote and staged the original musical *The Girl with the Red Balloon* at the University Cultural

Centre. The book was written by Aidan Woodford, and music by Liew Nam Yang and Ding Jian Han. Set in an old public Housing Development Board (HDB) estate which is due for demolition, the story is basically a love triangle. The male protagonist, Josh, defies convention by choosing to become an artist; but even his art is unconventional as he is a graffiti artist who paints on public area walls. Although Josh has garnered considerable acclaim, he remains unknown because he is hiding behind a pseudonym, GD. We feel sorry for him because we realise that his attempts to prevent the tearing down this old block of flats for redevelopment will be futile. We also learn about his attempts to salvage a broken relationship with his childhood girlfriend. Both missions seem doomed to failure. Josh's subtle and convincing character development is key to the success of this musical. Josh's childhood girlfriend, Indigo, has gone to New York for an extended internship, and has come back to Singapore only for a short visit. Josh's initial delight in seeing Indigo is quickly dashed when she introduces Howard, her fiancé, whose arrogant and condescending personality spurns Josh. What makes this musical so compelling is the in-depth development of the main characters. The music covers the entire spectrum of emotions including accompanying lively dances. *The Girl With the Red Balloon* is funny yet serious, it is frivolous yet profound, it is entertaining yet philosophical.

Pearls of Wisdom (2017)

Pearls of Wisdom was written by Brian Seward and music composed by Karen Lim. It was performed by children aged from 7 to 13 years attending St Andrew's Junior School. Several pearls are found in a large wooden box, each one representing a lesson to be learnt. They include understanding that building a life is like building a castle, and you should build it on solid rocks and not on soft sandy ground; you have to learn how to forgive debtors if they genuinely are unable to repay their loans; discovering that words of wisdom are like seeds for if you use them they will flourish if not they will wither and die; and finding out that your talents are like gifts in boxes and when you use them they will increase, but if you bury them they will rust away. The songs and dances complement the words of wisdom. The musical incorporates important life messages. *Make them Grow*, *Don't Hide Your Light*, and the title song *Pearls of Wisdom* are some of the memorable tuneful songs.

A Taste of Home (2018)

Students of Raffles Hall, National University of Singapore have written and produced one new musical every year, and the standard continues to climb. Scriptwriter was Alson Soh, the lyrics written by Teo Yuan Shao, Shannon Seet and Alson Soh, and the music composed by Thomas Gan, Clarice Low, Marcus Sim, and Kou Kai Seng. The story is about a declining Chinese restaurant run by a third-generation owner Ah Huat. A property investor, Ms Lin, is eyeing the building to purchase for future development. David, Ah Huat's son blames his father for the death of his mother, and the two always quarrel with one another whenever they meet. David has recently inexplicably quit his overseas job and returned to Singapore where he chances upon a former friend Michelle Lin, who assigns stars to her food blog, Michelle Lin Stars! Michelle is celebrating her birthday by cooking a meal and expects her mother to join her. But when mother fails to turn up, she quickly invites David, who fortuitously is able to accept at short notice. Over dinner you realize the pair are falling in love. Michelle tells of the distancing relationship between her mother and herself, and that creates a feeling of guilt in David. So the next day he decides to make up with his father Ah Huat, and the two revitalise the family restaurant. Michelle visits David at the restaurant and coincidentally property investor Ms Lin turns up to buy out Ah Huat. To Michelle's surprise, she realizes that Ms Lin is actually her own mother. She manages to persuade her mother not to buy the restaurant, and the two resolve their differences and hug each other. *A Taste of Home* displays the humor, the poignancy and the sadness of the story. The singing and dancing are top class. It ends with the performance of a waitress who was a former singer, and this brings in more customers that will keep the restaurant open.

Payback (2019)

The book and lyrics of *Payback* were written by Brian Seward, with music and lyrics by Karen Lim. The musical was performed by St Andrew's Junior School children 7 to 13 years of age. The story follows student Wallace and his 3 school friends and how they are led astray by super-villain Flatulardo and his sidekick Pong. Initially Wallace and his friends are idealistic and believe in doing good helping others without thoughts of reward. However, the super-villains want to degrade everybody in the world by making them become selfish and unwilling to help anyone else. Wallace and his friends find themselves in a different world where people speak in rhyme and will help only if they are paid with gold stars. Others refuse help suspicious that those who offer help are trying to cheat them. This behavior changes Wallace who adopts an egocentric uncaring attitude, and when he belittles his friend Luke, they separate. Pong wants to prove how fiendish he can be by making Wallace and his friends lose their altruism and he succeeds with Luke. But when it comes to Wallace, Pong's tactics backfire, and he regains his humanity. Wallace apologises to Luke and they become friends again, singing a moving song *Rainbow in the Clouds*. Together they and their friends persuade everybody that they should not accept payback rewards, but instead, they should pay it forward. This forms the jubilant finale song *Pay it Forward*. Everything works in this production.

A Perfect Life (2019)

Raffles Hall, National University of Singapore's students created the musical *A Perfect Life*. Erwin Cheng wrote the book, Gregory Tan and Erwin Cheng wrote the lyrics, Lim Zhen Heng, Lohsshini Sethu Pathy, Lim Ee Teck, and Bond Lee Chiang Eu wrote the music. The story revolves around five Raffles

Hall undergraduate students, each having personal problems, but hoping somehow that their problems can be solved. For example, Leanne comes from a poor family but wishes to get onto the Dean's List and win a scholarship which would greatly ease their family's financial burden; Lucas is a dancer who becomes paralyzed after an accident and hopes to be able to walk and dance again; and Joshua aspires to be able to express himself through music and to be able to sing. Their teacher Marilyn sets them an assignment: to write a musical. While working on the project, the students are kicked out of the library at midnight. They decide to go into a deserted room which is believed to be haunted. Unexpectedly, they stumble upon a magical wish-book, and they discover that by signing their names into the book, their deepest desires can be fulfilled. Miraculously, Leanne is placed on the Dean's List and wins a scholarship; Lucas can get out of his wheelchair and walk and dance again; and Joshua finds that he can sing very well indeed. What a perfect paradise! But slowly the five friends realize they are imprisoned in a concocted imaginary world with sinister undertones. The ruler is Evelyn, a doppelganger of their teacher Marilyn, who informs them that they can only be released from this world if they all agree to leave together, otherwise they are trapped in this musical world for the rest of their lives. Tough decision. The underlying question posed is whether it is worth deluding oneself and hiding from the truth. The production is first-rate, and it ends with a sensational finale song, *Trapped in a Musical*.

Home, Truly (2022)

The musical *Home, Truly* nearly got cancelled because two weeks before the production, half the cast came down with COVID-19. Luckily they recovered and all tested negative so the show could go on. Written by Raffles Hall, National University of Singapore's student Raynard Tay, the theme of *Home, Truly* is about how boarders living in a university hall of residence actually have two homes: Raffles Hall and one's own family home. The plot revolves around Axel, a bright-eyed freshman who is full of energy and wants to take part in as many societies as possible, including music and sports. But he has to balance time spent at the university and the expectations of his family at home, especially in taking care of his disabled wheelchair-bound sister. Things take a turn for the worse when Axel's father is badly injured at a workplace accident. His mother has to take care of father in hospital, and nobody is at home to look after his sister. Other frustrations encountered by Axel include when he is thrown out of the singing group by the brilliant but faultfinding perfectionist Roxane, and when his basketball rapper friends, the BackSeat Boys, play a joke on him which turns sour, Axel is on the verge of leaving the hall. Fortunately, a final year university friend, Henry, acts as a mediator and helps repair the fractured friendships, and brings everyone back together. The family joins the hall residents in singing the finale song *We are One Family After All*. This musical touches the audience, and one can see tears of joys in the final resolution.

7 Movie and Television Musicals

Introduction

Singapore used to have relatively few movie and television musicals. With the COVID-19 pandemic, cinemas and theatres were closed for about two years. Musicals that were going to be put on live stage had to be canceled, and therefore some of them were filmed and broadcast on television or the internet. Even converting a stage musical into film was difficult in the early years of the pandemic because of Singapore's restrictions limiting the number of people gathering together to be less than five, and the wearing of masks was compulsory. Added to the problem was that many institutions did not allow any filming in their buildings. However, an English opera titled *Panic Love* was initially planned to have been staged, but the pandemic forced it to be filmed and it was broadcast in 2020. Another musical written by students of the National University of Singapore was also converted from a stage production into a movie, titled *Rekindle*, and considering the difficulties the undergraduate students encountered, it was quite successful.

Before COVID-19, one of the more successful movie musicals was a Chinese-language film initiated and filmed in 2007 by Royston Tan, called *881*. In 2020, MediaCorp made a television series, Titoudao, based on the 1994 stage production of the wayang (Chinese street opera) musical with the same name.

Singapore's television company MediaCorp filmed and broadcast on television some children's musicals, including *School House Rockz* in 2008. This attracted good reviews and a fairly large audience, so MediaCorp commissioned a follow-up series in 2009, and after that they produced a full length movie in 2011, School House Rockz: the movie. They also decided to embark on another series of children's musicals titled *Witz* which was aired in 2011.

In India, Bollywood movies contain acting, singing and dancing, and we can consider them to be musicals. However, to date, Bollywood-style musicals are rarely made outside India. The popular Bollywood movie Devdas was converted into a stage musical and it premiered in Singapore in 2023.

Movie and television musicals is an area that has the potential to be developed much further in future.

881 (Film) (2007)

881
Royston Tan

Getai is the loud, garish live stage performance held annually during the Hungry Ghost (Seventh) Month of the Chinese calendar. In the 1970s the Singapore version of *getai* transitioned from Chinese Opera to modern day song-and-dance, sung mostly in Chinese dialects, especially Hokkien. *881* is a *getai* musical written and directed by Royston Tan with songs written by Funkie Monkies, Poh Tiong-Cai, and Robert Mackenzie. It follows two unrelated former classmates who attend a *getai* performance and were so enamoured by the artform they decided to join forces and sing together, calling themselves the Papaya Sisters; the word "papaya" sounds similar to the number "881." The taller of the two sisters is named "Big Papaya," to contrast with the shorter, who is named "Small Papaya." With the help of Big Papaya's aunt and her twin sister, the younger two sisters become *getai* performers, rapidly gaining huge popularity. Their rival is another pair of twin sisters known as Durian Sisters, who try to sabotage the Papaya Sisters. Initially they succeed by performing earlier and then blocking the

Papaya Sisters to get on stage. After some clashes, they decide to settle the rivalry by having a live competition. The champion is the pair that garners the most audience votes and they can then continue performing, while the losers would give up performing. The Durian Sisters lose, but in revenge they shoot spirit arrows, severely wounding the Papaya Sisters. The Small Papaya had been suffering from a serious illness, and she soon passes on. Big Papaya continues to perform together with her mother. The movie is produced by Royston Tan, and it is his tribute to the *getai* art form and to the older generation of performers. It was extremely popular and in 2011, the movie was adapted into a stage production.

School House Rockz Part 1 (2008) and Part 2 (2009)

School House Rockz the Movie (2011)

School House Rockz is a television musical series consisting of six episodes and broadcast in 2008. It was the brainchild of television and movie producer Yeo Lay Har. The script was written by Lynette Chiu and Raihan, and the music composed by Kenneth Lyen and Desmond Moey, with lyrics by Desmond Moey. The series revolves around Inka, a schoolgirl from a rich family studying in a high-class school. Her father feels that she has become too snobbish and transfers her into a less well-to-do neighbourhood school. Each episode deals with how she tries and nearly succeeds but eventually fails to extricate herself from the school. Stories include her being bullied by her classmates, quarrelling and injuring her during netball practice, persuading her to shoplift and then reporting her illegal act so she can be expelled from her current school. The songs are catchy and amplify the students' emotions, and they dance to the fast numbers. Following the success of the first series, a second series of six episodes was produced in 2009, and a movie with the same title was made in 2011. For the movie, the music and lyrics were written by Jack Ho and Rai Kannu (Jack and Rai) with additional music by Kenneth Lyen.

Rekindle (2022)

Rekindle is a movie musical entirely created by Raffles Hall, National University of Singapore. It is about a small group of rebels trying to evade a fictional brutally oppressive authoritarian regime referred to as the Imperium. This regime banned all forms of the arts, especially music. Alex is a lady singer covertly singing in a secret nightclub where she meets Edwin who has been given a pass to enter and it is his first visit to this underground club. He is immediately attracted to the singer Alex, and after her song, he offers to buy her a drink which she accepts. This is the start of a romantic love story that will travel along a tortuous route of twists and turns. It emerges that Edwin is a nephew of Imperium's dictator and is acting as a spy for his uncle William. But because he is in love with Alex, he helps her enter Imperium's highly guarded computer network to send an internet message to trigger a massive rebellion. It is understandable that owing to COVID-19 restrictions, certain limits to the filming were inevitable. For example, many outdoor scenes were prohibited, many institutions did not allow filming inside their building, and groups of more than five persons were disallowed. The overall tone of the musical was perhaps a little too serious, but ultimately *Rekindle* succeeds at many levels: as a gripping movie, as a musical with great songs, and as a biting satire. Raffles Hall's venture into the filmmaking of a musical is commendable.

References

1. 881 (2007 movie): https://en.wikipedia.org/wiki/881_(film)
2. 881 the movie Zhaowei synopsis. http://legacy.zhaowei.com/881/synopsis.html
3. Getai: https://en.wikipedia.org/wiki/Getai
4. School House Rockz (2008): https://www.imdb.com/title/tt15321928/plotsummary
5. Lyen K. Rekindle review (2022): https://kenlyen.wixsite.com/website/rekindle

8 Famous Personalities

A few selected prominent personalities who have made significant contribution to the musical theatre scene in Singapore are highlighted in this chapter. The individuals are chosen because of their active involvement in the establishment of major theatre companies or organisations, or their role in script or lyric writing or composing music for original Singapore musicals. This list is not complete, and perhaps future publications can expand on the individuals who have impacted Singapore's musical theatre.

Dick Lee (1956–)

Dick Lee is the most prominent and popular singer-songwriter and musical theatre composer in Singapore. He wrote the theme song for two National Day Parades, *We Will Get There* (2002), *Our Singapore* (2015), but is most known for *Home* (1998) which was also included in a National Day Parade. He has written his autobiography, some plays, directed the autobiographical film "Wonder Boy." As a songwriter, he has released more than 20 albums, and written many songs for Asian artistes.

Born of Peranakan heritage to Lee Kip Lee, a former president of the Peranakan Association of Singapore, Dick Lee is the eldest of a family of five. At home he listened to his father's jazz and big band music, while his mother enjoyed contemporary Western and Chinese pop songs. His secondary education was at St Joseph's Institution. He did not enjoy the school's academic subjects and performed poorly in the exams. He spent much of his time composing original music from the age of 12, which distracted him from his piano lessons. At the age of 15, he joined a vocal group called Harmony which took part in many talent competitions.

At the age of 17 Dick auditioned for a talent competition at Rediffusion, where he sung one of his own compositions, *Life Story*. Vernon Cornelius, the lead singer of the pop group Quests, was overseeing the auditions, and invited Dick to sing two of his original songs every week. This led to the release of his first album, "Life Story" in 1974. He championed the use of Asian elements in pop music, and this included the use of Singlish, (most notably in the hit song *Fried Rice Paradise*). Perhaps his most successful album was "The Mad Chinaman," which was released in 1989 and achieved platinum sales.

A year earlier, in 1988, Dick Lee wrote the musical *Beauty World* with a book by Michael Chiang. This was one of the early original Singapore musicals and has been restaged multiple times. Other musicals he wrote the songs for include *Fried Rice Paradise* (1991), *Nagraland* (1992), *Hong Kong Rhapsody* (1993), *Fantasia* (1994), *Kampong Amber* (1994), *Mortal Sins* (1995), *Sing to the Dawn* (1996), *Hotpants* (1997), *A Twist Of Fate* (1997), Jacky Cheung's acclaimed *Snow.Wolf.Lake* (1998), *Phua Chu Kang the musical* (2000), *Re-Mix* (2002), *Forbidden City: Portrait of An Empress* (2002), *Man of Letters* (2006), *Puteri Gunung Ledang* (2006), *P. Ramlee* (2007), *Fried Rice Paradise* (new version, 2010), *Lightseeker* (2013) and *LKY the musical* (2015).

Plays include *Death In Tuas* (1998), *The Good Citizen* (2004), *Beauty Kings* (2011) and *Rising Son* (2014).

Since 1998, Dick Lee has been the Associate Artistic Director of the non-profit Singapore Repertory Theatre which was founded in 1993.

Another area he exceled in was that of fashion design. He studied Fashion at Harrow School of Art and became involved in his mother's boutique where he designed clothes for his own labels. In the 1980s Dick formed "Society of Designing Arts" (SODA), which brought local designers together and introduced them to department stores, selling under their own names for the first time there. Local designer emporium "Hemispheres" was opened in 1986 to house local fashion. Dick was also the fashion editor for Female magazine in 1986, and owned model agency Carrie Models and fashion event company Runway Productions.

As a creative director, Dick has designed for Singapore's Christmas light-up, as well as headed creative departments at Mediaworks and Island Shop. He was also Vice President of A&R at Sony Music Asia from 1998 to 2000. Dick was appointed the Creative Director for Singapore's National Day Parade in 2002, 2010, 2015 (SG50), and 2019 (Singapore Bicentennial).

Among the many awards Dick Lee has won, are the 1995 Hong Kong Film Academy Awards for Best Original Movie Theme Song "The Search of My Life" for the movie "She's a Man, He's a Woman." In 1999 the Hong Kong Film Academy awarded him for the Best Original Movie Theme Song "No Longer in This Life" for the movie "City of Glass." Between 1998 and 2004 he won several of the Composers and Authors Society of Singapore (COMPASS) awards including an award for the Best Malay Pop Song. Dick was bestowed the Fukuoka Arts and Culture Prize in 2003, and in 2004 he won the Life! Theatre Awards for Best Music for his musical *Forbidden City*. That same year he received Singapore's highest art award, the Singapore Cultural Medallion.

References

1. Wikipedia: Dick Lee. https://en.wikipedia.org/wiki/Dick_Lee
2. Infopedia: Dick Lee. https://eresources.nlb.gov.sg/infopedia/articles/SIP_1595_2009-10-30.html

3. BiblioAsia: The music, madness and magic of Dick Lee. https://biblioasia.nlb.gov.sg/vol-11/issue-2/jul-sep-2015/dick-lee
4. Esplanade Off Stage: Dick Lee. https://www.esplanade.com/offstage/arts/dick-lee
5. Straits Times: Dick Lee: Shooting Wonder Boy was very emotional for me. https://www.straitstimes.com/lifestyle/entertainment/dick-lee-shootingwonder-boy-was-very-emotional-for-me
6. C. J. W.-L. Wee: Representing the New Asia: Dick Lee, Pop Music, and a Singapore Modern. in Transnational Asia Pacific: Gender, Culture, and the Public Sphere, ed. Shirley Geok-lin Lim, Larry E. Smith and Wimal Dissanayake (Urbana: University of Illinois Press, 1999), 117. (Call no. RUR 305.3095 TRA). https://www.cambridge.org/core/books/abs/house-of-glass/representing-the-singapore-modern-dick-lee-pop-music-and-the-new-asia/9895000BBEE6D779D7F88B453A466747

Stella Kon (1944–)

Stella Kon is a playwright who has also written the book and lyrics for several Singapore musicals. In addition she has written novels, short stories, and poems. Her most well-known work is the one-woman play, *Emily of Emerald Hill* which has been performed innumerable times in various countries, and was made into a musical in 2012.

She comes from a line of famous Peranakan Singaporeans. Her great-grandfather was the eminent Dr Lim Boon Keng who co-founded the Singapore Chinese Girls' School and the Oversea-Chinese Banking

Corporation. Stella's father was Dr Lim Kok Ann who was Professor of Microbiology at the University of Singapore, and Dean of the Faculty of Medicine. He loved listening to operas and watch theatre productions, and was known as the "Father of Chess in Singapore." Her mother was a sixth generation descendant of the famous Tan Tock Seng, who has a hospital named after him. Her maternal grandmother was Mrs Seow Poh Leng, who was the inspiration for the main character in Stella's play *Emily of Emerald Hill*.

Stella Kon was born in 1944 in Edinburgh where her father was studying medicine. In 1948 the family returned to Singapore and she lived in her grandmother's house at Emerald Hill. Her ancestry is Peranakan and Hokkien, but the main language spoken at home was English. Her mother studied for three semesters at the Royal Academy of Dramatic Art in London, and was a noted amateur actress as well as a teacher of literature and drama in Singapore. Stella watched her mother's performances, in rehearsal and on stage. As a result, Stella's earliest writings were plays for classroom production at Raffles Girls' School. Her sister Lim Sing Yuen became a jitterbug dancer of international fame, and two of her brothers are doctors, the third being a computer programme analyst. Her two sons are a radiologist and an orthodontist.

At the age of 6 years, Stella acted in *Trinity College Kindergarten* as Old Mother Hubbard. She studied at Raffles Girls' School where she wrote her first play, *The Fisherman and the King*, and her first published work, *Mushroom Harvest* which was included in a collection of short stories. She went onto the University of Singapore where she received a B.Sc. in Philosophy. In 2016 she receiveda Masters degree in Creative Writing from Nanyang Technological University.

Stella married in 1967 and moved to Malaysia, where she continued writing plays. Her collection of plays for students, *The Immigrant and other Plays* was published in 1975. Stella stayed in Malaysia for 15 years before moving to England where her sons went to school, and she returned to Singapore in 1987.

When Singapore's Ministry of Culture organised a National Playwriting Competition, Stella won the first prize three times, in 1979, 1982 and 1985, after which the competition was discontinued. The prize-winning play in 1985 was *Emily of Emerald Hill* which was first staged in Seremban, Malaysia in 1984.

Stella's first musical *Exodus* was written in 2003 in collaboration with the composer Kenneth Lyen. She went on to write two more musicals with Kenneth Lyen, *Blue Willow House* (2006), and *Monkey* (2009), a 60-minute puppet show. In 2005 Stella was a co-founding member and president of Musical Theatre Society which incubated new Singapore musicals, later incorporated as Musical Theatre Ltd, of which she remains a board member. In 2014 Stella was inducted into the Singapore Women's Hall of Fame. She wrote several more musicals including *Brand New Kind of Love* (2015), *Emily the Musical* (2017) which was based on her highly popular play *Emily of Emerald Hill*, and *My Love is Blind* (2017) based on the life of Tan Guan Heng, a pioneer champion of the visually impaired who was blind himself. In 2019 she wrote the musical *Lim Boon Keng* the musical, based on the life of her famous great grandfather. She wrote these musicals in collaboration with music composer and co-lyricist Desmond Moey.

Stella Kon is an important playwright, author and lyricist. Her play *Emily of Emerald Hill* is used as a textbook in Singapore schools and is the most produced play in the history of Singapore theatre. Through the arts charity she helped to found Musical Theatre Ltd, which actively supports the writing and production of new Singapore musicals.

References

1. Wikipedia: Stella Kon. https://en.wikipedia.org/wiki/Stella_Kon
2. Infopedia: Stella Kon. https://eresources.nlb.gov.sg/infopedia/articles/SIP_428_2005-01-14.html
3. Esplanade Off Stage: Stella Kon. https://www.esplanade.com/offstage/arts/stella-kon
4. Singapore Women's Hall of Fame. Stella Kon. https://www.swhf.sg/profiles/stella-kon/
5. Emily of Emerald Hill: Stella Kon. https://www.emilyofemeraldhill.com/about-stella-kon
6. Tan, Guan Heng (2008). 100 Inspiring Rafflesians, 1823–2003. World Scientific. p. 91. ISBN 9789812779465.
7. Musical Theatre Ltd. http://www.mtl.sg/

Iskandar Mirza Ismail (1956–2014)

Iskandar Mirza Ismail was an important musician in the early development of the Singapore musical. He was known as Singapore's "Music Man," who composed and arranged music, directed orchestras and choirs, produced recordings of performances, he was an inspiring educator with a good sense of humour.

Born in 1956 to a Singapore family at Kandang Kerbau Hospital, he was the eldest of five children, and they all lived in a kampong house which suffered regular floods. His parents were both singers. At the age of 6 years, Iskandar was learning the piano but admitted that he "hated practising." Nevertheless he had perfect pitch and his playing was good enough to be broadcast on Radio Television Singapore. When he was 8 years, he studied music under Zubir Said, the composer of Singapore's national anthem, and Iskandar described his piano lessons as "torture." At the age of 12 years, he started learning the Electone electronic keyboard, and at the tender age of 15, he was invited to teach at Yamaha Music School. In 1975 at the age of 19, he won first prize at the Singapore Electone Festival. Iskandar always wanted to be a pilot flying airplanes and he joined the Junior Flying Cloud. Unfortunately he was rejected from becoming a pilot when he "failed" a medical test. With the support of his family, he decided to become a professional musician. In 1976 at the age of 20 he was sent to the Berklee College of Music in Boston, where he won the John Lewis Jazz Masters Award in 1978. He graduated with a degree in Professional Music in 1978.

Iskandar composed the music for several of Dick Lee's musicals including *Kampong Amber* (1994), *Mortal Sins* (1995), *Sing to the Dawn* (1996), *Hot Pants* (1996), *A Twist of Fate* (1997), and *Snow. Wolf. Lake* (1997). He also arranged the music for Kenneth Lyen and Desmond Moey's musicals *Big Bang!* (1995), *Yum Sing!* (1999), and *Temptations* (2000). In 1997 he composed the music for Ekachai Uekrongtham's musical *Chang and Eng*. Iskandar was remarkably flexible in his music composition and performances, and was able to capture Malay, Chinese, as well as several Western styles of music. He composed music for solo as well as choral performances, and for single instrument as well as orchestral pieces.

From 1988 to 2012 he was involved in ten National Day celebrations. In 1997 he invited Kenneth Lyen and Desmond Moey to write the National Day song which he produced. In 2012 he composed the National Day song *Love at First Light*. From 2005 onwards he was deeply involved in the annual Child Aid concerts, and many of the young musicians who took part in these concerts are now outstanding professional musicians.

Throughout the years Iskandar Ismail received several awards including the prestigious Cultural Medallion Award in 2008 for his contribution to the Singapore music scene. His support for new musicals, orchestral works, as well as showcasing the talents of the young has had a lasting impact on the Singapore music scene. In 2010 Iskandar was diagnosed with lung cancer. Despite initial response to chemotherapy, the cancer spread to the brain and he succumbed in 2014. He is sadly missed.

References

1. Monica Gwee (2013): Iskandar Ismail: the music man. Published Epigram Books. ISBN 9789810768881
2. Wikipedia: Iskandar Mirza Ismail. https://en.wikipedia.org/wiki/Iskandar_Ismail
3. Koh A. Infopedia: Iskandar Mirza Ismail. https://eresources.nlb.gov.sg/infopedia/articles/SIP_2014-01-10_181916.html
4. Esplanade Off StageL Iskandar Ismail: Singapore's "Music Man". https://www.esplanade.com/offstage/arts/iskandar-ismail
5. Straits Times: Iskandar Mirza Ismail: talnted composer with laidback charm. https://www.straitstimes.com/lifestyle/entertainment/iskandar-mirza-ismail-talented-composer-with-laidback-charm

Goh Boon Teck (1971–)

Goh Boon Teck is a Singapore playwright, designer and director with a volume of theatrical works written in Chinese, English and other languages. He co-founded Toy Factory, a bilingual theatre company with a group of theatre practitioners and is currently its Chief Artistic Director.

Born in Singapore in 1971 of Hokkien ancestry, Goh Boon Teck's father was in the civil construction industry. His mother was a Chinese street opera (wayang) actress and naturally Boon Teck was brought along to watch his mother sing and act. It is through this exposure that he became fascinated by stage shows.

He is a graduate of the Nanyang Academy of Fine Arts in Singapore, and in 1990 he started his own theatre company, Toy Factory Theatre Ensemble (currently Toy Factory Productions Ltd). Among the many outstanding teachers who guided him was Singapore's theatre doyen Mr Kuo Pao Kun. In 1996, he was the first recipient of the VISA International Arts Scholarship which sponsored his studies in theatre directing in London.

In 1994 he wrote and directed the musical play *Titoudao* based on the life of his mother performing Chinese opera and the production went on to tour Cairo, Shanghai, Beijing, and Hangzhou. In 2001 this work won five Straits Times Life Theatre Awards for Best Play, Best Original Script, Best Production Design, Best Actress and Best Supporting Actor. In 2020, Titoudao was adapted into a television series broadcast on Mediacorp TV.

In 2001 Goh Boon Teck was conferred the National Arts Council Young Artist Award for his contributions to the development of Singapore theatre. At the age of 35, he was invited to be the Creative Director of Singapore's National Day Parade in 2007 making him the youngest director of this national event. He was invited back to be the Creative Director of the National Day Parade in 2008 and 2017. Boon Teck was also appointed as the Creative Director for the opening shows of Asia on the Edge Festival, organised by The Arts House in Singapore in 2008 and 2009. He was appointed as the Creative Director for Singapore Day in Shanghai in 2011.

In Singapore, Goh Boon Teck has concentrated on plays and musicals dealing with Asian heritage and culture. In 2009 he restaged the Singapore musical *December Rains* which he had originally watched in 1996. The following year, in 2010, he produced *Maha Moggallana* based on a Buddhist fable with cutting-edge costumes and modern dance. Other musicals he directed include *881* (2011) about a pair of *getai* singers based on the 2007 Royston Tan's movie musical of the same name. In 2014 he directed *Glass Anatomy*, a Singapore Mandarin musical which was staged at the Shanghai Cultural Square. He went on to produce the musical *Innamorati* (2017). He was also commissioned by the Singapore International Festival of Arts to direct the classic Ming dynasty trilogy *A Dream Under the Southern Bough* annually from 2018 to 2020. He has worked with many important figures in Singapore musical theatre including Elaine Chan, Bang Wenfu, Liang Wern Fook, Jimmy Ye, Philip Tan, August Lum and many others.

Goh Boon Teck's major achievements have been to create, produce and direct plays and musicals spoken and sung in Chinese for the Singapore stage.

References

1. Wikipedia: https://en.wikipedia.org/wiki/Goh_Boon_Teck
2. Esplanade Off Stage: Director's diary by Goh Boon Teck. https://www.esplanade.com/offstage/arts/directors-diary-by-goh-boon-teck
3. Goh Boon Teck Website: https://gohboonteck.com/about.html
4. TimeOut: Interview: Goh Boon Teck on 'Titoudao'. https://www.timeout.com/singapore/theatre/interview-goh-boon-teck-on-titoudao

Ong Keng Sen (1963–)

Ong Keng Sen is a Singapore artistic director of T:>Works (formerly known as TheatreWorks), one of the important theatre companies which helped launch three of Singapore's early musicals, *Beauty World*, *Fried Rice Paradise* and *Mortal Sins*.

Born in Singapore to Henghua-speaking parents from Fujian, China, Ong Keng Sen watched Cantonese soap operas in his childhood. He studied at the Anglo-Chinese School where he took part in the Literary, Debating and Drama Society. In 1984 he entered the National University of Singapore to study law, and became president of the Varsity Playhouse. Upon graduation he decided not to pursue a career in law, and instead he immersed himself into theatre. After being in theatre for about 30 years, he then did a Ph.D. in performance studies at New York University Tisch School of Arts in 2019. In 2022, he was awarded an honorary doctorate from the University of Arts London.

In 1988 he took up the post of artistic director of TheatreWorks where he directed Dick Lee's musical *Beauty World* with a script by Michael Chiang, and choreographed by Najip Ali. In 1991 he staged another Dick Lee's musical, *Fried Rice Paradise*. In 1992, he directed *Beauty World* which toured Tokyo, Osaka, Hiroshima, and Fukuoka. The next year he staged

Kuo Pao Kun's play *Lao Jiu* (1993), which was later adapted into a musical in 2005. In 1995, the whole artistic team of *Beauty World* reunited to create *Mortal Sins*, a musical about the real-life striptease artiste Rose Chan, and the show played to an audience of 20,000 at the Kallang Theatre. He then directed the movie version of Michael Chiang play *Army Daze* (1996), and he directed *Beauty World* for the President's Star Charity broadcast on television (1998).

Realising there is a lack of playwriting in Singapore, he started the annual Writer's Laboratory in 1990 to stimulate creative writing. From 1993 to 1994, he attended the New York University's Tisch School of the Arts to obtain a Master of Arts degree in Performance Studies. In 1995, he conceived of a biennale research and development programme named The Flying Circus Project which explores the Asian cultural expression of theatre, dance, music, visual arts, and film. This grew to include European, American, and Arabic artists and ran until 2013.

Ong Keng Sen was also known for revitalising the Singapore Arts Festival originally launched in 1977 to promote the performing arts in Singapore. In 2013, Ong Keng Sen was appointed the director, and he renamed the Singapore Arts Festival to Singapore International Festival of the Arts (SIFA). By 2017, he managed to attract an audience of 218,000 to this festival, which is a large number for Singapore theatre.

Through his role in promoting theatre arts in Asia, including Singapore, Ong Keng Sen received many awards, including the Young Artist Award (1992), the Cultural Medallion (2003) which is Singapore's highest arts accolade, and the Fukuoka Arts and Culture Prize (2010).

References

1. TheatreWorks archives: https://archive-tworks.org/the-flying-circus-project-2013/
2. Ong Keng Sen. Wikipedia: https://en.wikipedia.org/wiki/Ong_Keng_Sen
3. Nureza Ahmad. Infopedia: https://eresources.nlb.gov.sg/infopedia/articles/SIP_426_2005-01-13.html

Kuo Jian Hong (1967–)

Kuo Jian Hong is the Artistic Director of The Theatre Practice (Singapore) who has won awards for her theatre direction. In addition, she is also a lighting and set designer, and an independent film-maker. Kuo Jian Hong has taken on multi-faceted creative roles within the arts. Her extensive career spans over three decades, making her one of the key contributors to the development of the Singapore arts scene.

In terms of her artistic portfolio, she is best known for critically acclaimed local Chinese-language musical productions including *Lao Jiu* (2005), *If There're Seasons* (2007), and *Liao Zhai Rocks!* (2010). She also produced the play *Four Horse Road* (2020). These phenomenal works have brought new audiences to the theatres and nurtured a talented group of professionals involved both onstage and behind the scenes. Meanwhile, her passion for musical theatre and advocacy for the development of theatre for young audiences have led her to direct award-winning works such as *Day I Met the Prince* (1997) and *The Wee Question Mark* series (2017). This has also led to her spearheading *The Nursery Rhymes Project* (2017), a three-part initiative that seeks to rejuvenate the love for Chinese nursery rhymes among children today.

Kuo's repertoire includes experimental ventures. Her work *Blank Run* (2016) was invited to the World Stage Design in Taipei (2017). In 2018, she led a team of artists across the Chinese diaspora for *I Came at Last to the Seas*, a meditation on the fluidity of Chinese cultural identity. This was the first-ever full-commissioned undertaken by a local theatre company for the Esplanade Theatre at the Huayi Chinese Festival of Arts. Her work *Liao Zhai Rocks!* was invited to the Shanghai International Musical Festival (2019). Since 2020, Jian Hong has been leading the Theatre Practice team in developing hybrid digital and live theatre, pushing the limits of artistic innovation and technological capabilities with ambitious projects like *The Bride Always Knocks Twice — Killer Secrets*, a multilingual absurdist comedy staged in 2013 and again in 2021. She also created *Patch! A Live Theatre Festival of Play* (2020), a hybrid on/off line festival.

As the Artistic Director of Theatre Practice, Kuo's vision has allowed Theatre Practice to evolve with the times and emerge as one of the most progressive theatre companies in Singapore. Under her grassroots leadership, Theatre Practice continues to be a vital and relevant voice in the local arts scene, while charging ahead in its mission to always be a voice for the underdog.

Ivan Heng (1963–)

Ivan Heng is a theatre producer, playwright, actor, and he has produced several pantomimes and musicals. He also founded W!ld Rice, and is the artistic director of this theatre company.

Ivan Heng was born in Singapore (1963), a third generation Teochew whose ancestry came from Swatow in China, and English was spoken at home. He was educated at the Anglo-Chinese School and Temasek Junior College. He learnt to play the piano and passed Grade 6 of the Associated Board of Music. He also sung in school talentime competitions. In 1976 he was captivated by a cassette tape recording of the musical *A Chorus Line* and he imagined staging it. It was during his junior college days that he choreographed a dance performance and conducted the school choir. In 1977 he directed his first play *Wax* for the school drama festival.

During his National Service, he won a dance scholarship with Dance Arts Singapore in 1983. He went on to study law at the National University of Singapore, and during his undergraduate days (1984–1988) he attended Kuo Pao Kun's theatre workshop, acted in plays including Michael Chiang's *Army Daze* (1987), and designed the sets for the newly formed theatre company The Necessary Stage and directed the play *The Waiting Room*. Upon graduation he sung in Dick Lee's musical *Beauty World* (1988). This being one of the pioneer Singapore musicals, much of the rehearsal time was spent on experimenting with how to sing the songs with a variety of Singapore accents. Upon graduation from university, he was accepted to work in a law firm, but he soon decided to pursue a career in theatre.

In 1990 Ivan Heng obtained a scholarship to study at the Royal Scottish Academy of Music and Drama and he graduated as the top student in 1993. For the next few years, he worked in London in film, radio and television, and also toured Europe. In 1998 he decided to return to Singapore where he acted in the *Kiss of the Spider Woman* (1998).

Two years later, in 2000, he founded his own theatre company, W!ld Rice. He has since been producing a pantomime musical nearly every year, including *Cinderel-LAH*, *Jack and the Beansprout*, and *Peter Pan in Serangoon Gardens*. He also helped to produce *Dim Sum Dollies* musical comedies. He directed Julian Wong's *Don't Call Him Mr Mari Kita*, highlighting the songs written by Zubir Said, the composer of Singapore's National Anthem that begins with "Mari Kita."

In 2006, he was appointed the artistic director of the Singapore Theatre Festival, and in 2009 he was the creative director of Singapore's National Day Parade. He was the creative director of the Youth Olympic Games of 2010 in Singapore. He actively promotes theatre by conducting workshops both in Singapore as well as internationally. His theatre company W!ld Rice trains young actors in a programme that he started, called Young and Wild. His theatre company is also involved in the community.

Among the numerous awards he received, includes the Edinburgh Spirit of the Fringe award in 1995, the Singapore Young Artist Award in 1996, the Singapore Youth Award in 1998, the Straits Times Life Theatre Award for Best Director in 2002, and the Singapore Tatler Leadership Award for Culture in 2006. In 2013 he received the prestigious Cultural Medallion, Singapore's highest arts award.

Ivan Heng is an important figure in Singapore musicals as he creates original and entertaining pantomimes of such a high quality that they are re-classified as musicals. He also trains the young to be involved in theatre.

References

1. Wikipedia. https://en.wikipedia.org/wiki/Ivan_Heng
2. Prasad VJM. Infopedia. https://eresources.nlb.gov.sg/infopedia/articles/SIP_2014-10-28_163126.html
3. Liquisearch. https://www.liquisearch.com/ivan_heng/biography
4. W!ld Rice: https://www.wildrice.com.sg/
5. Alfian Sa'at. Twenty Years of W!ld Rice (2023). Epigram Books. ISBN: 9789814845885

Selena Tan (1971–)

Selena Tan is a theatre executive producer, director, playwright, comedienne, and singer. She has acted on the live stage, television sitcoms and movies. In 2000, she founded the theatre company Dream Academy.

Born in Singapore, she is the eldest of five siblings. Her father was an army officer and her mother was a gold broker. Selena went to St Theresa's Convent, Fairfield Methodist Secondary School and Raffles Junior College. Even in primary school, she was already singing songs from Broadway musicals. At the age of 14 years, she attended a theatre camp and came under the tutelage of the late theatre director Christina Sergeant.

In 1990, she was admitted to the National University of Singapore to study law, and during this period, she performed in theatre productions. Upon graduation in 1994 she entered the legal profession as a litigation lawyer but after three years of practice, she got a part in the Sondheim musical *Into the Woods* playing the role of Little Red Riding Hood. That same year she was in another musical, *Chang and Eng*, where she played the role of the mother of the conjoined twins. She also played a part in the MediaCorp TV drama *Under One Roof*. The year 1997 was a turning point in her life when she decided to quit the legal profession and become a fulltime actor.

As with many Asian parents, her parents were also concerned about their daughter's choice of an acting career, but Selena managed to convince them that this was her passion and destiny in life. Supported by her family, in 1999, she raised S$10,000 to stage her debut stand-up comedy *Selena Exposed*. The following year, Selena spent her life savings of S$13,000 to start her own theatre company, Dream Academy, which was devoted to the writing and staging of original comedies that comprised plenty of song and dance.

In 2002, Selena was having lunch with two of her drama colleagues, Pamela Oei and the late Emma Yong, and they decided to collaborate in a comedy production that incorporated a number of songs and a smattering of subtle political satire. This work explored the wacky Singapore culture and lifestyle, the unconventional use of blended language (Singlish), all done in good humor. The songs were original and written specially for the shows in a cabaret style. As the three friends were eating dim sum lunch one day, they decided to call themselves the *The Dim Sum Dollies*. One of the series was named *The History of Singapore* and portrayed an unconventional loose chronicling of Singapore's past. Sadly, Emma Yong passed away due to stomach cancer in 2012. Selena held a concert in her memory, and funds raised were donated to cancer and other critically ill patients.

Her most successful productions included the shows with the title *Dim Sum Dollies*, *Broadway Beng*, *Kumar the Queen*, *The Hossan Leong Show*, *Crazy Christmas*, *$ing Dollar* (the musical), and *Still Steam*.

Selena started her community service quite early in her career. In 2002 she led a project organised by W!ld Rice to produce plays and children's games in the void decks of neighbourhood housing and development board flats. She performed in concerts to raise funds for the Association of Women for Action and Research (AWARE). In 2012 she also organised a concert for the Singapore Kindness Movement to celebrate World Kindness Day. The following year, Selena was the creative director for the National Day Parade (2013). It differed from the usual production in that she used ordinary nonprofessional singers to sing the National Day song, and she also incorporated more music, dance and comedy into the celebration.

References

1. Wikipedia: Selena Tan. https://en.wikipedia.org/wiki/Selena_Tan
2. Lee XY. Infopedia: Selena Tan. https://eresources.nlb.gov.sg/infopedia/articles/SIP_2013-07-12_143321.html
3. Straits Times: My perfect weekend with Selena Tan. https://www.straitstimes.com/life/entertainment/my-perfect-weekend-with-selena-tan-founder-of-theatre-production-company-dream-academy
4. Dream Academy. https://www.dreamacademy.com.sg/
5. Wikipedia: Dim Sum Dollies. https://en.wikipedia.org/wiki/Dim_Sum_Dollies

Michael Chiang (1954–)

Playwright Michael Chiang is best known for his plays, musicals and screenplays, which are witty, satirical, and explore the cultural and social complexities of modern-day Singapore in a light-hearted way.

Born in Muar, Malaysia, he is the youngest of seven siblings. His father came from Hainan, and was the assistant headmaster at Muar High School, while his mother was a housewife who grew up in Seremban, Malaysia. Michael came to Singapore at the age of 11 and attended Anglo-Chinese School. As a child in the 1960s, he made regular visits to the cinema, watching mostly Hong Kong movies. During secondary school, he joined the literary and drama society, helping out backstage in theatre productions. He studied a combination of English Literature, Philosophy and Chinese Studies at the Singapore University, graduating with an Honours degree in Philosophy.

Michael became a journalist with The Straits Times Group in 1980, leaving after a decade to join the Singapore Broadcasting Corporation (later MediaCorp), where he was Chief Executive Officer of Caldecott Publishing, overseeing a stable of newsstand magazines that included best-selling titles like 8 Days, I-Weekly, Style, FHM, Elle and Manja. After 19 years at SBC/MediaCorp, he left in 2009 to start his own media and creative consultancy, A Little Imagination, where he took on various government projects. He was Co-Creative Director of *The Bicentennial Experience* (2019), Editorial Director of *The A List*, National Arts Council (NAC) print and digital fortnightly (2014–2018), as well as Editorial Consultant for Singapore Armed

Forces (SAF) *Pioneer magazine* (2009–2016). He was also scriptwriter for the National Day Parades in 2010 and 2014.

In 1984, while he was a journalist and was already known for his humorous comment pieces in The Sunday Times, he was invited to submit a light-hearted play for the Singapore Festival of the Arts. He came up with *Beauty Box*, a 25-minute spoof on beauty pageants and shopping, which delighted audiences but not critics.

In 1985, Michael Chiang wrote the book *Army Daze*, a tongue-in-cheek, "first-person" account of recruit life in National Service. In 1987, he was persuaded to write a stage version of *Army Daze*, and expanded the book into a comedy about five recruits. The play's box-office success is recognised as a significant turning point for local theatre, paving the way for Singapore-centric stories. *Army Daze* has since been restaged many times, and was made into a film in 1996, earning a record-breaking S$1.6 million for an English-language production. In 2017, he decided to revisit the original play and wrote *Army Daze 2*, a musical drama which traces the lives of the five recruits, 30 years on. This musical featured five original songs composed by Don Richmond.

Michael Chiang is also remembered for writing the script for the musical *Beauty World*, with songs by Dick Lee. Staged in 1988, the same year as *Makanplace*, both shows share the honor of being Singapore's premiere original musicals. *Beauty World* was restaged more than six times, and it also did a major tour of Japan in 1992, and made history as the first musical ever to be performed live on TV at the President's Star Charity in 1998.

In 1995, Michael Chiang wrote the book for the musical *Mortal Sins*, again with songs by Dick Lee. Despite its multimedia dazzle and controversial topic of Singapore censorship, the production somehow did not have quite the same audience appeal as *Beauty World*.

Michael's other plays include *Private Parts*, commissioned for the 1992 Singapore International Arts Festival, and *Mixed Signals*, which was adapted into a 13-part TV series in 2019/2020.

Michael Chiang is one of the pioneer writers of Singapore musicals and his comical satiric style opened up a more liberal perspective of Singapore's way of life.

References

1. Nureza Ahmad. Infopedia: Michael Chiang. https://eresources.nlb.gov.sg/infopedia/articles/SIP_423_2005-01-25.html
2. Wikipedia: https://en.wikipedia.org/wiki/Michael_Chiang
3. Esplanade Offstage: https://www.esplanade.com/offstage/arts/michael-chiang

Bang Wenfu (1974–)

Bang Wenfu is unassuming in nature, but he is one of Singapore's most preferred music producers, arrangers and composers.

He is of Hainanese heritage born in Singapore in 1974, the only son of a teacher father and a homemaker mother. He is married with a daughter. Wenfu started learning the piano at the age of 4 years, and quite early on he was found to have perfect pitch and strong music sensitivity. His music teacher was of the old school and reprimanded him whenever he played a wrong note. Instead of being suppressed, this stimulated him to become curious and he started to improvise playing more, which laid the foundation to his music compositions. He asked himself: "Why was I only playing the compositions of long-deceased composers (that) I had little interest in, and not given the blessings to develop my own compositions?" In the early days he was forced to follow the Associated Board of the Royal Schools of Music (ABRSM) syllabus and he was not interested in it. However, his parents forced him to complete piano grade 8 and theory grade 7.

Wenfu's interest in composing pop music developed during a school camp when he was 15 years old, and he was constantly asked to play hit pop songs from memory. He discovered his innate ability to remember tunes and chords, and so began writing music seriously from then on. At the age of 17, he received two years of music composition lessons from the late Leong Yoon Pin at the behest of his father. In 1992, he joined the Anderson Junior College choir as a piano accompanist. The conductor Thomas Kuek further fuelled his interest by making him his main accompanist for several of his school choirs, and let him transcribe popular musical numbers into choral arrangements.

During his national service he joined the Music & Drama Company (MDC) as a music accompanist for the Singapore Armed Forces Choir under Babes Conde. It was in MDC that he fully transformed himself into a professional musician.

Bang Wenfu went on to study at the National University of Singapore where he obtained a bachelor's degree in Arts and Social Sciences.

Upon graduation, Wenfu explored work in different schools, institutions and events companies. His musical abilities drew the attention of the late Iskandar Ismail who introduced Wenfu to musical theatre. In 1995 he was involved in the original Singapore musical *Big Bang!* From 1997 to 2012 he worked with Jonathan Lim in writing original parody songs for the annual Chestnuts show. He composed the music for the musicals *Chameleon* (2000), *Women on Canvas* (2000), *It's My Life* (2008), and *H is for Hantu* (2009).

He played important roles in several other musicals, including W!ld Rice's pantomimes *Oi! Sleeping Beauty* (2005), *Jack and the Beansprout* (2006), *Monkey Goes West* (2014), and Resorts World Sentosa's musical *Lightseeker* (2013). He was also involved in Chinese-language musicals produced by Theatre Practice that included *If There're Seasons* (2007), *Lao Jiu* (2012), *Liao Zhai Rocks* (2016), and Toy Factory's Chinese-language musical *December Rains* (2010, 2015),

Over the years, he has worked on a diverse range of other projects. For example, in 2007, he was the chief Music Director and arranger for the inaugural Singapore Day mega event in New York. He was also the designated music arranger for the 2014 Singapore Day event in London. He helped the late Iskandar Ismail arrange the theme song and closing ceremony theme of the National Day Parade in 2012.

In the pop music industry, Bang Wenfu has worked with Kit Chan, and he is well-known for his 20 years of collaboration with music producer Eric Ng, producing string arrangements for dozens of top-selling albums of Chinese pop artistes such as Stefanie Sun, Tanya Chua, Jolin Tsai, Sandy Lam, Fish Leong, and many others.

Bang Wenfu is also very active in promoting and producing musical theatre for schools. From 2001 onwards, he has composed, arranged and musical directed more than 30 shows in schools and colleges. At present, Wenfu has composed and arranged well over 500 pieces of music and is constantly evolving his style to cater for his clients' tastes. No wonder he is Singapore's most sought-after musician!

Elaine Chan (1971–)

Elaine Chan is a prominent Singapore music composer, arranger, piano accompanist and music director.

Elaine was born in Singapore to a Cantonese-speaking family. She is married and has two sons. She started learning the piano at the Yamaha Junior Music Course when she was five years old. Other instruments she played include the guzheng and the flute. At the age of eight she was selected to join the Yamaha Junior Original Course where she learnt music composition and arrangement. She went to Fairfield Methodist Secondary School (FMSS) where she joined the drama society and acted as Mrs Birling in her school play *An Inspector Calls*. She was an editor of the school magazine Fairsian Times, became the president of the school (FMSS) Choir, and she was also the school pianist. She received the Best Lyrics Award in the 1987 Chinese High inter-school songwriting competition. She went to the University of Texas at Austin to study music composition and obtained a bachelor's degree.

Elaine Chan worked with the late Iskandar Ismail in the musical *Chang and Eng*, and he inspired her and recommended her to be the vocal coach for the cast. Her classmate at Fairfield Methodist Secondary School was Selena Tan who founded Dream Academy and is one of the *Dim Sum Dollies* trio. She invited Elaine to be the composer, music director, arranger and pianist for many of their shows. Selena also introduced Elaine to Ivan Heng of W!ld Rice to be involved in their productions.

From 2003 she wrote the songs for W!ld Rice pantomime-musicals, including *Cinderel-LAH!* (2002, 2010), *Jack and the Beansprout* (2006, 2012), *Snow White* (2008), *Beauty and the Beast* (2009), *Hansel and Gretel* (2011), *Monkey Goes West* (2014), *Madam White Snake* (2017), *A Christmas Carol* (2019) and *Momotaro* (2020).

In 2010 Elaine Chan was involved in Sing'Theatre musical productions including *A Singaporean in Paris* (2010, 2014, 2022), *No Regrets* (2011), and *Quasimodo* (2022). She was also involved in several other musicals produced by other theatre companies, including Toy Factory's Chinese-language musicals *December Rains* (2010, 2015, 2022) and *881* (2011). She was the music director for the Singapore National Day Parade in 2005 and in 2013, and the vocal director of the Youth Olympics in 2010. In 2020 Elaine was commissioned by the Esplanade Theatre to compose music for the Malay stage musical *Alkesah*, and she composed the music for all 15 songs.

In 2023, Elaine performed in Sing'Theatre's *I Love You, You're Perfect, Now Change*; Toy Factory's musical *Ignite the Sun*, an original Mandarin-language musical commissioned by the Singapore Chinese Cultural Centre. She wrote the music for Dream Academy's *Sherlock Sam* (2023), and original music for Fairfield's Anniversary celebrations. In 2023 Musical

Theatre Ltd commissioned her to compose the music for *Unforgotten*. She was involved in the restaging of the classic *Cabaret* as well as W!ld Rice's pantomime *Snow White*.

Elaine Chan is involved in incredibly vast numbers of Singapore musicals, composing, arranging the songs, music-directing shows and vocal-coaching the singers, as well as being the accompanying keyboardist for almost all these productions. She has won several awards including the Composers and Authors Society of Singapore (COMPASS) Award for Artistic Excellence in 2017. She is certainly the musician in most demand in Singapore.

Gaurav Kripalani (1971–)

Gaurav Kripalani is the artistic director of the Singapore Repertory Theatre, and was the director of the Singapore International Festival of the Arts (SIFA) from 2017 to 2021.

He was born in Calcutta in 1971, studied in Singapore, and started acting in primary school at the age of 10. When asked which musical instrument he played he said he played the radio! He attended Raffles Institution where he joined the Raffles Players drama club which inspired him to enter an acting career. His family was very supportive when he told them he wanted to go into theatre studies. He pursued a double degree, a bachelor of arts in theatre and dance, and a bachelor of science in political science at Santa Clara University, USA. During his freshman year he spoke to one of his professors for two hours, and was offered an acting role in Shakespeare's Tempest. This experience reinforced his calling into a life of theatre.

Upon graduation he joined a lobbying firm in the USA, and after that he came back to Singapore to work in a software company. A five-hour long meeting with Tony Petito, the director of the Singapore Repertory Theatre (SRT) led to his being offered the role of a teacher in Dick Lee's musical *Sing to the Dawn*. This was in 1996 and was his first experience working in a professional theatre company, and he learnt self-discipline and time management.

When Tony Petito returned to the USA, Gaurav took over as director of SRT. He introduced a broad range of different works ranging from *Shakespeare in the Park* and other plays, to mounting original Singapore musicals. He was involved in *A Twist of Fate* (1997) which was the opening show for the Singapore Arts Festival. On the first day of rehearsal for that show, everyone was sitting in a circle, getting ready to introduce each other, when Gaurav turned to his left and introduced himself. The very friendly gentleman said "hello" and nothing more. So he followed up with "And you are?". The answer was: "I'm Dick Lee, I wrote the music for this show." Gaurav was mortified for not recognising Dick Lee, but fortunately, they became firm friends and went on to produce six more musicals together.

The other Dick Lee musicals Gaurav produced were *Forbidden City: Portrait of an Empress* (2002), *Re-Mix* (2002), and *LKY* (2015). In the 30 years of his career, Gaurav has produced over 100 shows, of which 20 are musicals. However, managing a theatre company can be quite difficult in Singapore, and it is often a struggle to keep a company afloat. Gaurav initially had to give up acting in order to manage SRT. He believed in being very ambitious producing high quality shows and courageously risking the possibility of "crash and burn."

Gaurav was appointed director of SIFA in 2017 but then the COVID-19 pandemic started in 2020, resulting in the closure of theatres for a year and even when they were reopened, audience size was severely restricted. He worked very hard to revive SIFA as well as SRT. Indeed it was during the recovery phase of the COVID-19 pandemic that he returned to acting in 2021 when he performed in SIFA's play *The Commission*, the first-ever collaboration between SRT, W!ld Rice and Pangdemomium. His advice to anyone who wants to pursue a career in the performing arts: "Don't do it." But if that person is foolish enough to enter this world, they must have absolute commitment and unwavering passion. He also advocates revamping the educational system and to introduce the arts to the young to allow them to develop their talents.

Gaurav stated his vision for Singapore saying: "Our goal is to create the great Singaporean musical that we can tour around the world and fly the Singapore flag."

Liang Wern Fook (1964–)

Liang Wern Fook was born in Singapore to a Chinese press journalist father and an acupuncturist mother. He was bathed in music at home and he enjoyed singing Chinese and English songs. He played the piano and passed the Associated Board grade 8 exam. At the age of 16 he lost a debating competition which pricked him into composing his first Mandarin song. In Catholic High School he wrote several Chinese poems and essays for which he won several prizes. At Hwa Chong Junior College he continued writing many songs. He went on to read Chinese Studies at the National University of Singapore and he carried on composing and singing. He graduated in 1988 and was a gold medallist in both Chinese Studies as well as in the Arts and Social Sciences.

It was while he was in college in the 1980s that Taiwan folk songs were entering a golden era, which influenced Wern Fook into composing a new form of Mandarin ballads. He began writing the Chinese lyrics together with original melodies and these songs became very popular in Singapore. They were named *xinyao*, meaning "Singapore songs," and Wern Fook is credited as the most prominent pioneer of this musical style. The songs are described as having a clear melody and the vocalists sing in harmony usually accompanied by a guitar. A prolific songwriter he released his first album in 1986 titled *Mun* (Door), followed shortly by four more albums and selling over 20,000 copies which is considered astronomical for Singapore.

In 1992, after releasing his last album, he shifted his focus and became an academic. He got a Masters degree in Chinese from the National University of Singapore in 1992, followed by a PhD from the Nanyang Technological University (NTU) in 1999. He became an associate professor at NTU where he mentored students in creative Chinese writing and literature.

In 1996 Liang Wern Fook decided to enter musical theatre and he wrote the book, and co-wrote the songs with Jimmy Ye, for the musical *December Rains*. He achieved a double first because not only is it Singapore's first Chinese musical, but it is the world's first to incorporate *xinyao* music and this musical was restaged in 2010 and 2015. In 2003, Wern Fook wrote a song titled *If There're Seasons* and it won the MediaCorp Radio FM93.3 Award. A few years later in 2007, he took this song and used it as a title song for his next musical, which was also very successful and was restaged in 2009 and 2014 with all shows sold-out. In 2010 he was awarded the Singapore Cultural Medallion for music, and in 2021 he was conferred the Singapore Cultural Contribution Award for his outstanding contributions to the promotion, enrichment, propagation and development of Chinese Singaporean culture.

References

1. Liang Wern Fook. Wikipedia. https://en.wikipedia.org/wiki/Liang_Wern_Fook
2. Liang Wern Fook. Infopedia. https://eresources.nlb.gov.sg/infopedia/articles/SIP_2014-03-11_160318.html

3. Xinyao. Wikipedia. https://en.wikipedia.org/wiki/Xinyao
4. Xinyao. Infopedia. https://eresources.nlb.gov.sg/infopedia/articles/SIP_2015-02-17_175438.html

Desmond Sim (1961–)

Desmond Sim is a Peranakan Singaporean writer of plays, short stories, movies, book and lyrics for musicals, poetry and he is also a painter.

He was born in Singapore in 1961 and was educated at St Gabriel's School, the National Junior College and in 1982 he went to the National University of Singapore (NUS) to study English Literature. In 1985 he was awarded a Japan Airline scholarship to study Japanese theatre and art history in Tokyo. That same year, he won the ACBC Gold Medal for Literature given by NUS. He then did a Master of Arts degree in literature at NUS and in 1991 he was awarded a scholarship by the Fulbright Professional Programme to study theatre and poetry in USA, and he participated in theatre and poetry programs across the country.

In 1991 Desmond started his own communications consultancy Desmond Sim & Co. Pte Ltd. Later, he merged his firm to a design group, The Green House Group, where he was appointed executive director. The multi-disciplinary Group offered exhibitions and graphic design, marketing and corporate communications. The Group was acquired by Frontline Technologies in 2002.

In 1990, after winning both the first and second prizes at the Shell-NUS National Playwriting competition, Desmond Sim was invited by Ong Keng Sen to work for a year as Singapore's first full-time paid Playwright-in-Residence at T:>Works (formerly TheatreWorks). He helped to start the Writers Laboratory, which is now in its 33rd year promoting young writers. His earlier works that were selected up for production by T:>Works include *Blood and Snow*, and *Sammy Won't Go To School*.

He won the first prize in Action Theatre's very first Hewlett-Packard/ Action Theatre 10-Minute Play Competition in 1993. Subsequently, three of his 10-minute plays were staged in December 1993: *Elizabeth by Night* performed by the Actors Theatre of Louisville in the USA, *Drunken Prawns* (1994) and *The Drowning Place* (1994) staged by Action Theatre. *Kampong Amber*, a 1993 musical by Music & Movement and directed by Glen Goei, was Desmond's first commission to dramaturg for a musical, while *A Singapore Carol*, a 1994 premier production with the Singapore Repertory Theatre, was his first full-length adaptation of a Charles Dickens story into a Singapore context.

In 1995, Desmond Sim wrote the script for *Corporate Animals*, an Action Theatre collaboration with Ekachai who directed it and Ken Low who wrote the songs. He subsequently wrote the book and lyrics for two more musicals, *Jack and the Beansprout* (2006) with W!ld Rice, and the puppet musical *Pinocchio* (2017).

Desmond has written over 40 plays, with over 30 of them produced in Singapore, Malaysia and the USA. He has received numerous accolades for his work. He won the Merit Prize in 1993 for the Singapore Literature Prize for Poetry, and he won the Best Play and Best Original Script award at the Straits Times Life Theatre Awards in 2002. He has taught playwriting for Action Theatre for more than a decade, and he has taught at Lasalle College of the Arts, and currently he is teaching at Mindchamps Academy of Stars. He has published two anthologies of plays with Epigram Books, and his plays are also performed and studied by schools, junior colleges and tertiary institutions.

In short, Desmond Sim is a notable individual whose works continue to inspire the development of theatre and literature in Singapore and beyond.

Jonathan Lim (1974–)

Jonathan Lim is a writer and director of plays, revues, videos and musicals. He is also a singer and actor.

He went to Catholic High School, Tampines Junior College and he entered the National University of Singapore for theatre studies. He won a scholarship to the National Institute of Dramatic Art in Sydney, Australia where he studied directing.

Jonathan Lim is best known for his annual satirical revues under the series Chestnuts. Occasionally his jokes are a little bit too edgy for the Singapore board of censors and they have curtailed some of the language used. He wrote the book and lyrics for musicals, pantomimes and a musical opera. They include: *Women on Canvas* (2000), *Oi! Sleeping Beauty* (2005), *Jack and the Beansprout* (2006), and *H is for Hantu* (2009), *Aladdin* (2011), *Pursuant* (2013), and *A Singapore Carol* (2018). He directed the musical *Temptations* (2000), and he created *Kursed* (2019), a live interactive horror experience in an abandoned kampong.

In addition to writing the book and lyrics for musicals, Jonathan is credited with screenwriting for the telemovie *+65*, writing the lyrics to Royston Tan's film *Cut* (2004), and to Eric Khoo's feature film *In the Room* (2015), as well as for the sitcom *Meet the MP* (2017–2019). He has also written a book about the Chinese supernatural landscape in Singapore, *Between Gods and Ghosts* (2005).

Jonathan is multitalented and he is known for his ability to explore unorthodox beliefs to challenge conventional boundaries.

Dezz Desmond Moey (1959–)

Dezz Moey is a prominent songwriter who has written the music for several musicals and composed the National Day Theme Song in 1997.

Dezz was born in Singapore in 1959 to Cantonese-speaking parents. He graduated in engineering at the National University of Singapore and went on to do a Master's degree in mass communication. He learnt to play the guitar and sing, and liked to listen to songs especially by John Denver.

Dezz Moey started collaborating in musicals with Kenneth Lyen in 1995. He wrote the songs to *Big Bang!* (1995), *Yum Sing!* (1999) *Temptations* (2000), MediaCorp TV series *School House Rockz* (2007), *A Christmas Wish* (2008), *Esther* (2008), *Lost in Transit* (2009), *Monkey* (2009), MediaCorp TV series *Witz* (2011), *So You Want to be a Nurse* (2012), *Superhero* (2013), *Samoga Bahagia* (2015), *Emily* (2016), *My Love is Blind* (2017), *Lim Boon Keng* (2019), and *Peter and Pierre* (2022).

Dezz Moey has also been invited to compose numerous songs, including the school songs for the Rainbow Centre and Pathlight School, and the opening of Fusionopolis attended by Prime Minister Lee Hsien Loong (2009), Celebration of Singapore International Water Week (2014), and for many commercial corporations.

He teaches music and lyric writing at Republic Polytechnic, and he also helped in developing campus musicals at the National University of

Singapore. He is one of the founders of Musical Theatre Ltd which promotes the writing and staging of new musicals.

Chen Zhangyi (1984–)

Chen Zhangyi is a prolific music composer in opera, choral, chamber and orchestral works. He is also a conductor, violinist, violist and educator.

Born in 1984 to a Hokkien father in the electronics repair business who plays the *dizi*, and a Teochew homemaker mother. Zhangyi is the middle child of three brothers. At the age of nine, his mother enrolled him to learn the classical violin. He joined the choir during his secondary school days at Anglican High and junior college at Temasek Junior College. He went on to study music composition at the Yong Siew Toh Conservatory of Music, gaining a bachelor's degree in 2009. He then went on to obtain a master's degree in music composition and theory at the Peabody Institute in Baltimore, Maryland in 2012, followed by a doctorate in composition with a minor in conducting and baroque violin in 2015.

When he returned to Singapore, Zhangyi joined the Yong Siew Toh Conservatory of Music (YST) in 2015 to teach, and he is currently an Assistant Professor in music analysis and composition. His compositions are extensive and they include a symphonic work *Of An Ethereal Symphony* for the Singapore Symphony Orchestra's European Tour in 2016, a violin concerto *Vanda* for the Singapore Symphony Orchestra's National Day

Concert in 2018, and a 'Triple' Concerto for Erhu, Ruan, Percussion and Ensemble 《三人行》 for the YST Orchestra's tour to Korea in 2019.

Zhangyi has written the music for seven chamber operas. This includes *A Singapore Trilogy* (2018) which combines *Laksa Cantata* (2012, 2018), *Window Shopping* (2014), and *Kopi for One* (2018) with libretto by Jack Lin. His other operas include *Panic Love* (2020) *a cappella* opera with libretto by Felix Cheong, *Kampung Spirit* (2021) opera with libretto by Sara Florian, and *Arianna On Another Island* (2022) children's opera with libretto by Sara Florian. His latest opera *A Day A Lily — Part I* (2022) was presented in the form of a docu-opera, with libretto by Jack Lin, directed by filmmaker Lim Ziyu.

Zhangyi was conferred the Young Artist Award by the National Arts Council of Singapore in 2014, which led to a studio recording of *A Singapore Trilogy* released through United Records. His work *Ariadne's Love* won the Abbey Road Studios Anthem Competition, and was recorded by the London Symphony Orchestra accompanied by the Eric Whitacre Singers.

Chen Zhangyi is Singapore's most prominent opera composer. BBC Radio 3 described Zhangyi's works as "music from a voice of the future."

Joel Tan (1987–)

Joel Tan is a Singaporean playwright based in London and Singapore.

He was born in 1987 to a nurse, and a Hainanese father working in a maritime company, and he is the middle child of three siblings. He graduated from the National University of Singapore, and pursued a Masters degree in Dramatic Writing at Central Saint Martins in London.

Joel has written several musicals. In 2013 he wrote the book and lyrics for W!ld Rice's musical-pantomime *Jack and the Beansprout*, followed in 2015 by writing the lyrics to *The Emperor's New Clothes*. In 2017 he wrote the lyrics for the musical *Tropicana* supported by the Singapore Tourism Board. He wrote the libretto for the opera *Butterfly Lovers* that was staged in Melbourne (2022) and Singapore (2023).

Joel Tan has written a number of plays produced in Singapore by Checkpoint Theatre, and Pangdemonium Theatre, and in London by Theatre503, Orange Tree Theatre, Royal Court Theatre, and others. Some of his notable plays include *Family Outing* (2011), *The Way We Go* (2014), *no particular order* (2018, 2021), *Love in the Time of Ancients* (2019), *When the Daffodils* (2021), *It Matters, How We Say Goodbye* (2021), *Living Archive* (2022). His earlier plays have been compiled into one volume and published in 2016, and some of his more recent plays have also been published separately.

His play *Café* was nominated for the Straits Times Life Theatre Awards for Best Original Script in 2017, and his play *Tango* was nominated for the Life Theatre Awards for Best Original Script in 2018, and his play *Love in the Time of Ancients* was shortlisted for the Papatango Prize in London 2019.

Joel Tan also works inter-disciplinarily, and has collaborated with visual artists, poets, musicians and dancers as a writer, director and dramaturg. He wrote a live immersive audiotour for London's Chinatown, known as *Augmented Chinatown* (2021, 2022).

In addition to his work as a playwright, Joel Tan is also an educator through organising workshops and mentoring young theatre practitioners. He is a Creative Associate with Centre 42's New Writing Development Programme, and runs its Professional Development Residency for playwrights.

Joel Tan's writings explore complex themes such as identity, family, and social justice. His works have been performed in Singapore and internationally.

Julian Wong (1988–)

Julian Wong was educated at New Town Secondary School and Concord College in England. He learnt to play the piano and violin, and received further training in music arrangement and orchestration from several prominent Singapore music teachers including the late Iskandar Ismail, Sylvia Khoo and Belinda Foo. When Belinda Foo became the music director of

Theatre Practice she roped him in as a rehearsal pianist and keyboardist for their productions in 2008 and 2009, and in 2010 he took over as music director. Julian furthered his studies at Berklee College of Music where he did a Bachelor of Music in Professional Music. During this period, he took a major course in piano and a minor in conducting.

Julian Wong's introduction to musical theatre was by Iskandar Ismail in the musical *Chang and Eng* when Julian was only 11 years old. That year he also watched Mark Chan's musical *Haunted* and was enraptured by the music which he could remember by heart. Later, he worked with Mark Chan for about five years and was asked to help in the Singapore Arts Festival 2012. In 2008 he wrote songs for a short musical called *Singapore Boys* produced by Musical Theatre Ltd's project "Five Foot Broadway." W!ld Rice then asked Julian to develop the musical into a larger work and it was renamed *Botak Boys* and performed at the Singapore Theatre Festival in 2008.

Between 2008 and 2017 he worked with Brian Seward in his theatre company I-Theatre, writing original music for several children's shows including *The Ant and the Grasshopper*, *The Enormous Turnip* and *Under the Baobab Tree*. The latter was performed at the Edinburgh Fringe Festival (2011). He wrote *Magic Porridge Pot* which was performed in the Petaling Jaya Live Arts (2014).

In 2015 Julian Wong was asked by Joel Tan and Pam Oei to write the music for a pantomime, but at that time he felt that pantomimes were not up to the standard of traditional musical theatre, so initially he turned down the invitation. However, Ivan Heng managed to persuade him to compose for the pantomime *The Emperor's New Clothes* (2015) which broke out of what he perceived to be mere low-level slapstick entertainment. Julian also wrote *Pinocchio* which was a very moving and quite a philosophical interpretation of an old story. He now prefers not to refer to these productions as pantomimes but rather as musicals. He said, "I certainly don't think of them as pantomimes."

Since 2016 he has been teaching music at the Institute of Technical Education. "My students keep me grounded because they are unimpressed and could not care less about my work! At the end of the day, I see myself most as a music teacher. I love music and theatre, but I don't like the business of it. I have always found my personality incompatible for the industry."

Julian has many achievements, including being granted the National Arts Council Arts Scholarship (2012). He has won many awards, including the Alex Ulanowski Award, the Outstanding Service Award, the Professional Music Excellence Award, and the Piano Department Achievement Award, all from Berklee College of Music (2012–2013). He is an upcoming important personality in shaping the future of the Singapore musical.

References

1. W!ld Rice: The music man. https://www.wildrice.com.sg/newsletter/NL29/article04.html
2. The A-List: An interview with Julian Wong. https://www.a-list.sg/an-interview-with-julian-wong-the-musical-mind-behind-dont-call-him-mr-mari-kita/
3. TimeOut: Julian Wong Plays with Fire. https://www.timeout.com/singapore/things-to-do/julian-wong-plays-with-fire

Developing New Singapore Musicals

Introduction

Musicals are an important art form. It differs from non-musical theatre in that musicals require cast members to act, sing, and they may also have to dance. What music does is that it adds an extra dimension to the emotions experienced and one can understand the characters more deeply.

The benefit of writing and producing new musicals is that it is a highly creative collaborative art form. The writing part involves thinking of a good storyline, scripting good lyrics and composing great music. Other members of the creative team include the producer, the director, the choreographer, the music arranger, the costumes and set designs, the lighting and sound engineers. The list goes on much further.

Musical theatre bonds people together and friends are often formed with people from a wide variety of talents and expertise. This is particularly apparent in school and tertiary institution productions. It inspires many to go on and become creative in their lives.

Musicals tell different stories, ranging from retelling historical events to fables and imaginary worlds. It often delves into philosophical and ethical issues in an understandable format.

One advantage Singapore has over the West End and Broadway is that the cost of a production remains relatively low, although it has been rising recently. A reasonably good production can be mounted for around $750,000. This contrasts with the multimillions of dollars that is often spent for one show in the USA, Europe and Australia. The theatres in Singapore where musicals are usually performed, are relatively new and are equipped with state-of-the-art acoustics and stage facilities. However, assembling the right team of producers, directors, choreographers, performers, musicians, lighting and sound designers and stage managers remains a perennial problem. It must be remembered that the Singapore musical only started in 1988 and virtually from scratch. Over the past few decades, production companies have gradually built up their expertise. This is an ongoing evolution and remarkable progress continues to be made.

What is the future of musical theatre in Singapore? How can we encourage the production of more original musicals? Below are some possible routes to take.

Incubating New Musicals: Musical Theatre Limited

In an effort to forge a more systematic developmental process, an association called Musical Theatre Society (later renamed Musical Theatre Ltd) was set up in 2004. Founding members include Stella Kon, Desmond Moey and Kenneth Lyen. This organisation helps discover new creative talents and finds collaborators for writers, composers, and the other members of the production team. It nurtures talent by inviting experienced playwrights, composers and directors to critique and mentor the creative teams. Readings of the embryonic musical are conducted in front of small groups, and when ready for public display a staged reading is performed in front of an invited audience that includes producers from established theatre companies who are invited to take up the work for commercial staging. To date, this organisation has incubated over 30 new musicals, including *Georgette* by Ng Yi-Sheng and Clement Yang, about the life of Singapore artist Georgette Chen. This musical was staged in Singapore and the Philippines in

2007. There have been several experimental short musicals, like *10 Days of Mourning* by Carolyn Camoens, who is active in the Singapore Indian arts scene. This musical featured traditional Indian music composed by Nawaz Mirajkar in 2006. Another experimental musical from 2006 was *The Swami, the Cow and the Spaceman* by Musa Fazal, with music by Sean Wong.

Training Young Performers

In 2008 children aged between 13 to 18 years interested in the music and theatre can choose to go to the School of the Arts (SOTA) where they can focus on music, dance and theatre. Between the ages of 17 to 18 years, students can enrol in the Nanyang Academy of Fine Arts and LaSalle College of the Arts to study music, dance and theatre. However only LaSalle offers a special musical theatre course leading to a degree. Already this musical theatre course is playing an important role in supplying well-trained performers, technicians and administrators in musical theatre.

Most of the major theatre companies in Singapore have a section devoted to engaging young performers. W!ld Rice has Young & Wild, Singapore Repertory Theatre has The Young Company, Dream Academy has Dream Stage Kids. To help train more musical theatre performers, a number of primary and secondary schools are now promoting the production of school musicals. Toy Factory works with some of the schools. These are important avenues to give first-hand experience which can foster greater interest in theatre.

Campus Musicals: Schools, Polytechnics, Universities

Currently only a few schools write new original musicals. One of the schools, the Anglo-Chinese School has engaged their students to write the script, the lyrics and compose the music for new musicals that are staged in the school. Students from the National University of Singapore (NUS), Nanyang Technological University and Yale-NUS have also engaged their students to create and perform their own original musicals.

The most consistent creators of new annual musicals are the final year law students, and residential college students of Raffles Hall, both of the NUS. The undergraduates write the book and lyrics, and compose the music, choreograph the dance, and design the sets and costumes for their annual musicals. During the COVID-19 pandemic Raffles Hall students managed to write two film musicals, but since 2022 they have returned to performing the musical on stage.

Indeed there is a lot of talent in schools and tertiary institutions and with appropriate support and stimulus, it will generate creative writing and provide an environment that will forge lifelong friendships. Some of the students who have taken part in these campus musicals have gone on to continue writing or performing in musicals after graduation. Others have formed new groups to write original musicals in community centres and other organisations.

Musical Writing Competitions

Singapore has several songwriting and playwriting competitions. Although international musical theatre writing competitions can be found overseas, this rarely takes place in Singapore. Musical Theatre Ltd did attempt to have a modest "competition" showcasing a series of short 10-minute musicals from 2005 to 2010, but this has not continued. It is suggested that the National Arts Council should sponsor musical theatre writing competitions. Hopefully this will spur more people to write new musicals. Let us have a look at selected examples for Singapore and international songwriting and playwriting competitions.

Songwriting Competitions

Some people require an incentive to prod them to become creative, and success in a songwriting competition can have financial and publicity returns. Winning can also help connect with other music professionals as well as add to one's reputation. Writing a song might require a team comprising a music composer, lyricist and an arranger, and a competition can forge these links. It is important that participants should remember that winning does not guarantee future success, and that it is the kick in the posterior that spurs one into action, which is the main purpose for entering the competition. Upon realising that it is a competition, songwriters are motivated to keep on improving the melody, the lyrics, and the music arrangement. The two major languages used for songwriting competitions are English and Chinese. The latter includes the *xinyao* Chinese style of music, which remains quite popular. So far Singapore songwriting competitions do not have any entry fee, so there is no monetary deterrent.

Playwriting Competitions

In Singapore, playwriting competitions are almost all restricted to completing a new play within 24 hours. Before the COVID-19 pandemic, all the playwrights were assembled into a large building with access to food, drinks, and toilet. The participants are supervised and given encouragement if they have stopped writing, and they are prevented from cheating by communicating with outsiders. Both young and old from all walks of life enter the competitions.

The oldest 24-hour playwriting competition was started by TheatreWorks in 1996. In 2008, the company partnered with the SouthEast Community Development Council. More recently it has linked up with ArtsRepublic.sg which is a free online listing magazine dedicated to promoting Singapore arts, and founded in 2009.

Festivals

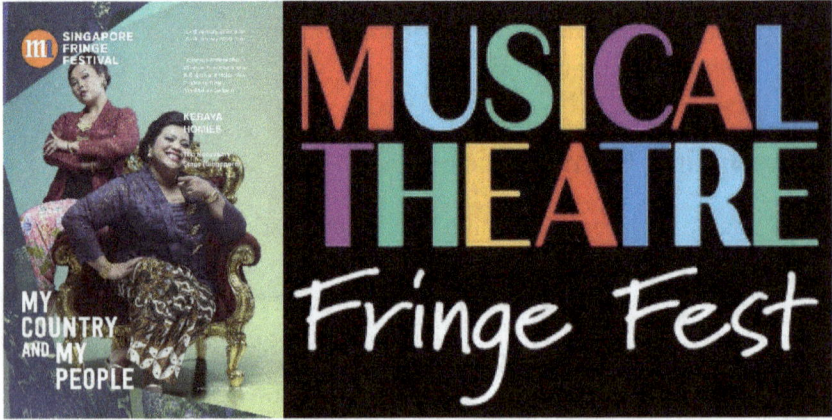

Singapore has many festivals of the arts that promote musicals and other art forms. One of the most popular is the Singapore International Festival of Arts (previously Singapore Arts Festival) which was started by the National Arts Council in 1977. It is an excellent platform for showcasing new works.

Other festivals include The Necessary Stage's annual M1 Fringe Festival started in 1987 that has been producing theatre, music, dance, visual arts and mixed media, created and presented by Singaporean and international artists. Another festival for promoting musical theatre is the Sing'Theatre's Fringe Festival staged musicals, conducts workshops, talks and events. In 2022 it presented the new musical *Tissue Aunty*.

Arts festivals are beneficial because they spur more creative writing and productions, and some of the new musicals produced are quite innovative.

Modern Technology

Many theatre companies are worried that modern technology can negatively affect the development of new stage musicals. There are several reasons why there is this fear. For example, virtual reality headsets will allow one to experience the musical as if one were inside the space where the musical is taking place. The audience need not physically go to a theatre to see a show. They can use the special headsets and watch the show at home. Those who have visited the Van Gogh immersive exhibition will understand that to wander inside the painting gives one a much deeper appreciation of the painting. Add to this an ability to touch, feel, and move the sets, and this is what augmented reality can achieve.

The second fear is that artificial intelligence (AI) will be able to write future musicals. Yes indeed, AI has already generated an entire musical which was staged in London in 2016. Intelligent computers wrote the book, composed the music and supplied the lyrics to create an entire original new musical titled *Beyond the Fence*. Being the first AI musical, some critics lambasted it, while quite a number of audience members said that it was not bad for a first attempt. Will AI write better musicals in the future?

AI has also written pop songs that nobody seems to be able to tell the difference whether it is written by a computer or a human. This will almost certainly change the way that songs are generated, and together with the spoken script, musicals created by computers will compete with humans.

However, with new technologies, there may be benefits. Perhaps the ability to harness AI to generate better quality musicals may attract a larger audience. Or perhaps it may create new forms of musicals that we currently are unable to conceive? Only time will tell.

Conclusions

Musicals marry several artforms together, including acting, singing, and dancing. The skills of writing the book and lyrics, composing the music, choreographing the dance, designing the stage and costumes and directing the actors require a high degree of creativity. To be successful, the teams need to work closely with each other, and that helps bond them into closer friendships.

Musical theatre in Singapore is fresh and energetic. It is influenced by both the West and the East, and in time, will find its own unique voice. But the future of the Singapore musical depends on the creation of many more new works, on audience development, on increased corporate and government support, and further liberalization in the attitudes of the general public and the funding bodies.

A successful show will not only attract local audiences but will also draw in people from overseas, just as Broadway and the West End attract tourists from all over the world. Some Singapore shows have even been able to travel overseas. Thus musical theatre has the potential to show the world that Singapore possesses artistic and creative talents. It paints an impressive picture of a small country that balances the sciences with the arts. Indeed throughout history, many famous scientists are also good artists and musicians. To quote Ivan Heng, artistic director of W!ld Rice, "Musicals are a wonderful form of entertainment and escapism. The best ones are those which tell our stories and hold up a mirror to our times."

As mentioned above, artificial intelligence (AI) has already written an entire musical staged in 2016. But will AI replace human writers and composers of musicals? Not if we keep one step ahead of it. When used thoughtfully, modern technology and artificial intelligence can be harnessed to boost creativity, generating more original innovative and exciting musicals, and enhancing one's experience of the creations.

The final message is that musical theatre serves several functions. It generates creativity, promotes teamwork, it is holistic education, a wonderful form of entertainment, and it can give profound insights into our inner soul. We must not abandon this art form, and we must continue our spirited support for the future.

Musicals embody our humanity.

References

1. Musical Theatre Ltd. https://mtlmanager.wixsite.com/mtl5
2. Singapore School of the Arts (SOTA). https://www.sota.edu.sg/
3. Nanyang Academy of Fine Arts (NAFA). https://www.nafa.edu.sg/
4. W!ld Rice. https://www.wildrice.com.sg/
5. Singapoe Repertory Theatre (SRT). https://www.srt.com.sg/
6. Dream Academy. https://www.dreamacademy.com.sg/
7. Toy Factory. http://toyfactory.com.sg/
8. Necessary Stage. https://www.necessary.org/
9. Sing'theatre. https://singtheatre.com/shows-singtheatre/

Songwriting Competitions

10. Singapore Youth Festival: https://yuhuapri.moe.edu.sg/singapore-youth-festival-syf-songwriting-achievements/
11. National Schools Xinyao Songwriting Competition: https://www.moe.gov.sg/news/press-releases/20201123-winners-of-the-xin-kong-xia-national-schools-xinyao-songwriting-competition-2020
12. Singapore Chinese Cultural Centre Dream Composition Songwriting Competition: https://singaporeccc.org.sg/events/22nd-xqrj-the-dream-composition-song-writing-competition-grand-finals/
13. Mandopop I Write the Songs Songwriting Competition: https://singaporeccc.org.sg/events/22nd-xqrj-the-dream-composition-song-writing-competition-grand-finals/
    5 USA: https://www.musicalwriters.com/career/2018-awards-for-musical-theatre-writers/
14. USA National Endowment for the Arts: https://www.arts.gov/initiatives/musical-theater-songwriting-challenge
15. International Songwriting Competition: https://songwritingcompetition.com/

Playwriting Competitions

16. TheatreWorks Arts Republic 24-hour Playwriting Competition. https://www.artsrepublic.sg/events/2022/07/24-hour-playwriting-competition-2022
17. Singapore Chinese Cultural Centre Gimme 10! Radio Playwriting Competition (Mandarin): https://singaporeccc.org.sg/events/gimmeten/

Artificial Intelligence

18. AI Composed Songs https://www.cbc.ca/radio/thecurrent/the-current-for-june-21-2018-1.4715519/this-pop-artist-used-artificial-intelligence-to-compose-an-entire-album-1.4715571
19. Top 10 AI Music Composers https://filmora.wondershare.com/audio-editing/best-ai-music-composer.html
   https://showbizzwoman.com/can-a-computer-create-an-amazing-musical-with-ai/
20. Margaret. ShowBizzWoman (2021) Can a computer create an amazing musical with AI? https://showbizzwoman.com/can-a-computer-create-an-amazing-musical-with-ai/
21. Pringle A. New Scientist (2016). Beyond the Fence: how computers spawned a musical. https://www.newscientist.com/article/2079483-beyond-the-fence-how-computers-spawned-a-musical/
22. Deshpande N. TheOdysseyOnline (2015). Beyond the Fence: the computer-generated musical. https://www.theodysseyonline.com/beyond-the-fence-musical
23. Beyond the Fence the musical written by AI https://www.youtube.com/watch?v=IzeSDloI-7I&t=357s

Index

A $ingapore Carol, 75
Act 3, 8
Action Theatre, 13, 27, 144
Adeeb Fazah, 47
Adeline Tan, 25
Admiral Cheng Ho, 27
Adrain Oh, 12
Aidan Woodford, 103
Aladdin, 66
Alec Tok, 38
Alfian Sa'at, 70–72, 74
Alkesah, 58
Alson Soh, 104
Alvin Chiam Hwee Chin, 56
Andrea Teo, 34
Andrew Lloyd Webber, 51
Anthony Drewe, 17
A Perfect Life, 106
Arianna On Another Island, 90
Army Daze 2, 134
AR Rahman, 51
artificial intelligence, 159
A Singapore Trilogy, 85
A Taste of Home, 104
Atlas Unbound, 100
A Twist of Fate, 16
August Lum, 60

Babes Conde, 136
Bang Wenfu, 19, 21, 30, 68, 135
Beatrice Chia-Richmond, 32
Beauty & the Beast, 70
Beauty World, 1, 3, 9, 116
Belinda Foo, 149
Bennett Bay, 47
Beyond the Fence, 159
Big Bang!, 12
Bombay Dreams, 52
Bond Lee Chiang Eu, 106
Brian Seward, 19, 101, 103, 105, 150
Bunga Mawar, 82

campus musicals, 95, 156
Catherine Casey, 25
Catherine Lim, 11
Centre 42's New Writing Development Programme, 149
Chameleon, 19
Chang and Eng, 3, 5, 15
Checkpoint Theatre, 149
Chen Yang, 60
Chen Zhangyi, 84–86, 88, 89, 91, 147
Chestnuts, 145
Chong Tze Chien, 30, 43
Chu Ben Wee, 100

Cinderel-LAH!, 66
Clarice Low, 104
Clement Yang, 29
Corporate Animals, 13

Darren Ng, 43
December Rains, 53, 142
Denise Marsh, 19
Desmond Moey, 12, 20, 26, 39, 45, 111, 120, 122, 146, 154
Desmond Sim, 13, 43, 68, 143
Devdas, 52
Dick Lee, 1, 9–11, 15, 17, 23, 24, 34, 36, 51, 115, 122, 125, 129, 134, 140
Dilwale Dulhania Le Jayenge, 52
Dim Sum Dollies, 131, 138
Ding Jian Han, 103
Don Richmond, 32, 134
Dream Academy, 131, 155
Dream Stage Kids, 155
Dwayne Lau, 77

Ed Gatchalian, 37
Edmund Ooi, 25
Edwin Thumboo, 82
881 (Film), 110
881 Musical, 57
Elaine Chan, 32, 58, 62, 66, 68, 70–72, 74, 75, 77, 137
Emily, 39
Emily of Emerald Hill, 118
Emma Yong, 131
Empress Dowager, 23
English language musicals, 7
Eric Khoo, 145
Eric Ng, 38, 57, 137
Erwin Cheng, 106
Exodus, 96

famous personalities, 115
Felix Cheong, 88, 90, 148
Fences, 83
Festivals, 158
Firefly in the Light, 99
Five Foot Broadway, 150
Forbidden City: Portrait of an Empress, 4, 5, 23
Frankie Malachi Yeo, 31, 43, 58
Frankie Yeo, 19
Fried Rice Paradise, 10, 116
Funkie Monkies, 110

Gaurav Kripalani, 139
George Chan, 57
Georgette, 29
Georgette Chen, 29, 38
Glen Goei, 144
Goh Boon Teck, 51–53, 57, 60, 62, 123
Gregory Tan, 106

Hansel and Gretel, 71
Haresh Sharma, 41
Haunted, 17
Henry Chua, 25
H is for Hantu, 30
Hoang Du'c, 96
Hoh Chung Shih, 90
Home, Truly, 107
Ho Minfong, 15
Hoon Ding Yi, 98

If There're Seasons, 5, 56, 142
Ignite the Sun, 62
Inconvenience of Minor Parts, 90
Incubating New Musicals: Musical Theatre Limited, 154
Iskandar Ismail, 20, 54, 121, 136, 149

Index

I-Theatre, 150
It's My Life, 30
Itsy, 43
Ivan Heng, 65, 91, 128, 151
Ivan Ho, 22

Jack and Rai, 112
Jack and the Beansprout, 68
Jack Ho, 112
Jack Lin, 85, 86, 148
Jason Tan, 32
Jean Tay, 27
Jimmy Ye, 53
Joel Bertrand Tan, 41
Joel Tan, 69, 73, 76, 78, 91, 148, 150
Joel Trinidad, 36
John Sharpley, 83
Jonathan Lim, 21, 30, 67, 68, 75, 84, 136, 145
Jonathan Price, 55
Jonathan Shin, 102
Joshua Chua, 96
Julian Chua, 40
Julian Wong, 41, 65, 73, 76, 78, 149
Justin Kan, 33

Kampong Amber, 10
Kampung Spirit, 89
Karen Lim, 97, 101, 103, 105
Keep the Flame, 100
Ken Low, 13, 15, 27, 144
Kenneth Lyen, 12, 19, 20, 22, 33, 96–98, 111, 112, 120, 122, 146, 154
Kevin Seah, 40
Kit Chan, 137
Klaus Kristian, 98
Kopi for One, 87
Kou Kai Seng, 104

Kuo Jian Hong, 51, 55–57, 60, 127
Kuo Pao Kun, 55, 129

Laksa Cantata, 85
Lao Jiu, 3, 55
LaSalle College of the Arts, 144, 155
Leon Foo, 40
Leow Siak Fah, 83
Liang Wern Fook, 51, 53, 56, 141
Liao Zhai Rocks!, 57
Liew Nam Yang, 103
Life Story, 116
Lightseeker, 34
Lim Boon Keng, 45, 118
Lim Ee Teck, 106
Lim Yu-Beng, 30
Lim Zhen Heng, 106
LKY Musical, 4, 35
Lohsshini Sethu Pathy, 106
Lo Pei-An, 60
Lost In Transit, 26
Lynette Chiu, 111

M1 Fringe Festival, 158
Maha Moggallana, 124
Makanplace, 1, 8
Making the Grade, 97
Mama White Snake, 74
Marcus Sim, 104
Mario Chan, 46
Mark Chan, 17, 150
Mark Richmond, 32
Matthew Leong Yoon Pin, 82
MediaCorp Studios, 26
Meira Chand, 36
Michael Chiang, 9, 125, 132
Mindchamps Academy of Stars, 144
Ming Wong, 15
modern technology, 159

Momotaro and the Magnificent Peach, 77
Monkey Goes West, 72
Mortal Sins, 13
Mr Beng, 54
Musical Theatre Ltd, 29, 39, 40, 45, 120, 147, 150
musical writing competitions, 157
Music & Drama Company (MDC), 136
Music & Movement, 144
My Love is Blind, 40

Nanyang, musical, 37
Nanyang Academy of Fine Arts, 155
Ng Swee San, 97
Ng Yi-Sheng, 29
Non-English Musicals, 51

Oi! Sleeping Beauty!, 67
Ong Keng Sen, 125, 144
Oon Ah Chiam, 52
Opera Viva, 83
Otto Fong, 54
Ovidia Yu, 17

Paiseh Pieces, 47
Pamela Oei, 131
Pam Oei, 150
Pangdemomium, 141
Pangdemonium Theatre, 149
Panic Love, 88
Pantomimes, 65
Payback, 105
Pearls of Wisdom, 103
Peter Casey, 26
Peter Pan in Serangoon Gardens, 76
Phua Chu Kang, 25
Pinocchio, 42, 78

Playwriting Competitions, 158
Poh Tiong-Cai, 110
Pursuant, 84
Puteri Gunung Ledang, 4, 51

Quek Yee Kiat, 62

Raihan, 111
Rai Kannu, 112
Raymond To, 56
Raynard Tay, 108
R. Chandran, 8
Rekindle, 112
Re:Mix, 24
Rene Ong, 55
Richard Lord, 98
Richard Mills, 91
Robert Mackenzie, 110
Robert Yeo, 83
Robin Loon, 25
Roulette, 98
Royston Tan, 57, 110, 145

Sara Florian, 89, 91, 148
Sayang, 22
school and university musicals, 95
School House Rockz, 111
School House Rockz the Movie, 111
School of the Arts (SOTA), 155
Sean Cheong, 96
Sebastian Ang, 102
Selena Tan, 32, 66, 130
Shannon Seet, 104
Shanty, 25
Shayna Toh, 99
Singapore Festival of Arts, 10
Singapore International Festival of the Arts (SIFA), 126, 139, 158

Singapore Lyric Theatre, 82
Singapore Repertory Theatre, 10, 15, 17, 139, 155
Singapore's Lyric Opera, 84
Singapore's "Music Man", 121
Singapura, 4, 36
Sing Dollar!, 31
Sing Theatre, 138
Sing'Theatre Musical Theatre Fringe Fest, 159
Sing to the Dawn, 4, 14
Sleepless Town, 32
Snow White and the Seven Dwarfs, 69
Snow Wolf Lake, 3
Society of Designing Arts (SODA), 117
Sometime Moon, 3
Song of the Whale, 95
songwriting competitions, 157
So You Want to be a Nurse, 33
Stella Kon, 26, 39, 45, 97, 118, 154
Stephanie Phang, 47
Stephen Clark, 15, 23, 36
Stephen Hawking, 12
Stephen Yan, 12
Steven Dexter, 16
Sylvia Khoo, 149

T:>Works (TheatreWorks), 9, 17, 25, 125, 144, 158
Tan Beng Tian, 55
Tan Guan Heng, 40
Temptations, 20
Teo Yuan Shao, 104
The Admiral's Odyssey, 27
Theatre Practice, 127, 150
TheatreWorks, 9, 17, 25, 125, 144, 158

The Butterfly Lovers, 91
The Emperor's New Clothes, 73
The Finger Players, 43
The Flying Circus Project, 126
The Girl with the Red Balloon, 102
The Huiying, 98
The Magic Paintbrush, 18
The Necessary Stage, 158
The Quests, 25
The Soldier and His Virtuous Wife, 60
The Theatre Practice, 55
The White Hare, 59
The Young Company, 155
Thomas Gan, 104
Thomas Lim, 76, 78
Tissue Aunty, 46
Titoudao, 52
Tony Petito, 16, 35, 140
Toy Factory, 32, 52, 123, 138, 156
Training Young Performers, 155
Tropicana, 41

Victoria Opera, 91
Vincent Wong, 22
virtual reality headsets, 159
Viva Lah Singapura!, 101
Vivienne Lin, 25

Window Shopping, 86
W!ld Rice Theatre Company, 65, 91, 129, 132, 138, 150, 155
Women on Canvas, 21
Wonder Boy, 116
Writers Laboratory, 144
Wu Xi, 55

Xiaohan, 38, 55, 57
xinyao, 142

Yang Qian, 55
Yeo Lay Har, 111
Yong Siew Toh Conservatory of Music, 147
Young and Wild, 130, 155
Yvonne Alain Lek, 98

Zhang Fan, 62
Zhang Xian, 55
Zulfadli Rashid, 58

www.ingramcontent.com/pod-product-compliance
Lightning Source LLC
Chambersburg PA
CBHW070309230426
43664CB00015B/2694